Man of 55/60.
Height: 1.65m.
Osteoarthritis and
scoliosis. Arterial
atheroma. Bandages
perfectly preserved.

KU-160-088

Well-built man of 40/45. Height: 1.70m. Probable cause of death: bilharzia. Major part of bandages preserved.

Slender woman of
35/40 with long
curly hair.
Height: 1.53m.
Cause of death:
bilharzia.

Well-built man of 50.
Height: 1.70m.
Osteoarthritis and
scoliosis.

Well-built man of
40/50. Height: 1.63m.
Osteoarthritis and
scoliosis.
Compression fracture
of two vertebrae.
Bilateral
dysplasia of hip
and femur.

Man of 40/45. Strong build contrasting with slight stature (1.51m). Probable cause of death: bilharzia. Osteoarthritis and scoliosis.

Woman of 60.
Height: 1.57m.
Decalcified bones
and poor dental
 condition;
    advanced osteo-
       arthritis;
        prolapsed
          womb.

Woman of 60 with
short dyed hair.
Height: 1.49m.
Osteoarthritis
and scoliosis.
Decalcified bones
(probably post-
menopausal).
Probable cause of
death: cranial
fracture.

8 2 5 8 1 1 7

Man of 45/50. Height 1.56m. Probable lithiasis of the bladder (possible cause of death). Nostrils widely dilated by insertion of linen plugs (now lost).

CONTENTS

MUMMIES
A JOURNEY THROUGH ETERNITY
Françoise Dunand and Roger Lichtenberg

THAMES AND HUDSON

Travellers of antiquity marvelled at the strange country which, as Herodotus, writing in the 5th century BC, said 'did everything differently from everyone else'. While the Greeks cremated their dead, the Egyptians attempted to preserve in theirs the semblance of life. Thanks to such records, and those of Arab travellers, the West has always thought of Egypt as the land of mummies.

CHAPTER 1

THE DISCOVERY OF THE FIRST MUMMIES

The 17th-century image of mummies was still fanciful, as in della Valle's, *Examination of mummies at Dahshur*, 1674. Left: Belzoni's lithograph *The Great Chamber in the second pyramid at Ghizeh*, 1818 is a more accurate record.

Mummies were among the 'wonders' discovered by the first Europeans, precursors of the modern-day tourist, who ventured along the banks of the Nile in the 15th century.

It quickly becomes fashionable for travellers to take back souvenirs: statues, amulets and even coffins complete with their occupant

In 1605 a Frenchman named du Castel bought a mummy and two sarcophagi in Cairo. Several decades later the poet La Fontaine, seeing them in the home of Nicolas Fouquet, the wealthy financier and patron of the arts, was prompted to write: 'The coffins or tombs of King Chephren and King Cheops have been shipped here recently (not without effort and expense) in great haste from a strange land'. (A completely fanciful identification, we should add.) The painter Sir Peter Paul Rubens also owned one, which he used as a model for a number of drawings.

From the 16th century, powdered mummy, known as *mumiya*, was regarded as a universal panacea and was found on apothecaries' shelves. Trading in mummy became a lucrative business and inevitably led to the manufacture of false *mumiya* to meet growing demand.

Two major events marked the beginnings of Egyptology – the scientific study of ancient Egypt. In 1798, the Directory gave Napoleon Bonaparte leave to assemble an army and invade Egypt. This enabled the young general to fulfil his oriental dream. The military operation itself was a fiasco, but Napoleon had the brilliant idea of taking with him a group of experts whose job it was to produce an exhaustive inventory of the country's monuments and of its flora and fauna. The result was the massive *Description of Egypt*, first published in 1809.

In 1822, in a letter dated 27 September to M. Dacier, permanent secretary of the Académie des Inscriptions et Belles-Lettres in Paris, the young scholar Jean-François

The first *Description of Egypt* (1735), was based on the memoirs of Benoît de Maillet, French consul in Egypt (1692–1708). The above illustrations taken from it (left: an open coffin revealing the bandaged mummy; right: a mummy case) are fairly accurate. However, the pyramids and sphinx at Giza (top right) in *Les Voyages et Observations du Sieur de la Boullaye-le-Gouz* (1657), are much more schematic. The sphinx, whose head alone was visible above the sand, is labelled Ablehon, a distortion of its Arab name, Abu el Hul, meaning 'the father of terror'.

Champollion (1790–1832) – who had not taken part in Napoleon's expedition – announced that he had succeeded in deciphering Egyptian hieroglyphs. Thanks to this major linguistic breakthrough the land of the pharaohs was to emerge from fifteen centuries of silence.

Europe in the grip of Egyptomania

Motifs inspired by ancient Egypt invaded the decorative arts, architecture and interior furnishings. Collections, both public and private, were enriched with a wealth of Egyptian artifacts. To meet the growing demand, pillaging of ancient sites increased and mummies and sarcophagi were regularly shipped over to Europe. Not all survived the journey: the sarcophagus belonging to the 4th-Dynasty pharaoh Mykerinus, for example, went down with the ship which was carrying it to England and now lies somewhere in the Mediterranean.

Scene of a Napoleonic soldier supervising the transport of a mummy (below), a detail from a painting by Léon Cogniet for Charles X. The painting is in the Louvre, on the ceiling of the Campana room designed to house Champollion's Egyptian collection.

Egypt discovered

On 19 May 1798 10,000 sailors and 36,000 soldiers set sail from Toulon for Egypt. With them was a team of mathematicians, astronomers, engineers, naturalists, artists and printers armed with Arabic, Greek and Latin characters. For two years they studied everything, from the quality of Nile water to mirages and the possibility of linking the Red Sea with the Mediterranean (the future Suez Canal). Their principal interest, however, was Egypt's past. The result was the massive *Description of Egypt* from which these watercolours, above and left, are taken. Above: a human ear, probably part of a funerary mask; left: funerary statuettes known as ushabtis. The hieroglyphs have been perfectly reproduced, although no one could yet decipher them.

A painting by Léon Cogniet (far left) for the Campana room in the Louvre.

The richest museum in the world

The *Description de l'Egypte … publiée sur ordre de S. M. l'Empereur Napoléon* was designed to be an exhaustive study of Egypt at the time of the Napoleonic expedition. Along with detailed descriptions of the ancient monuments and antiquities (left and far left) it aimed also to provide an inventory of contemporary flora and fauna (scientific research overlapped here with economic interest). It was also a systematic survey of ethnographic and geographic features. The work, in nine volumes of text and eleven of illustrations, comprising 907 colour plates and more than 3000 illustrations, took almost twenty years to complete.

Many Egyptian antiquities ended up in museums as donations by private collectors. In fact, only a tiny minority of mummies was shipped abroad compared to the number left in Egypt. Of those that did remain, however, few were safe from pilfering hands. Looters in search of jewels and amulets overlooked by their ancient predecessors had no scruples about stripping their victims or even tearing them to pieces. Nor were animals spared: throughout the 19th century England imported hundreds of tons of mummified cat for the sole purpose of manufacturing fertilizer.

Mummies were initially regarded as no more than objects of curiosity, but over time interest assumed a more scientific slant. During the 19th century meetings were organized to mark the ceremonial unwrapping of mummies. Often the only point was to collect some item of value, but, as if to give the operation scientific credibility, a brief description was sometimes drawn up.

In 1908 Margaret Murray (wearing an apron), of the University of Manchester, conducted the clinical investigation of an adult male mummy dating to the 12th Dynasty (1991–1783 BC). The mummy was discovered in the course of official excavations carried out by the great English archaeologist Sir William Flinders Petrie (1852–1942) in Lower Egypt. After 1858 no sites could be excavated or antiquities exported without the permission of the Antiquities Service in Cairo.

'**When I see, and touch, the bodies of so many illustrious persons we never imagined could be more than names to us … I still find it hard to believe that I am not dreaming**'

'Where I had expected to meet one or two petty kings,' continues Gaston Maspero (1846–1916), director of the Egyptian Antiquities Service, 'the Arabs had uncovered a whole vault full of kings. And what kings!' Packed in together in a cache at Deir el-Bahari, Maspero had discovered the most famous pharaohs of the New Kingdom (1550–1070 BC) – Amosis I, Tuthmosis I, II and III, Amenophis I, Ramesses II and III and Seti I – along with their queens – Nefertari and Aahotep among them – and numerous princes and princesses as well as major court officials. This fabulous discovery came about as a result of a cross between a police investigation and an eastern fairy tale.

The appearance of royal burial goods on the antiquities market during the previous decade or so had attracted archaeological attention. Maspero began making enquiries in Luxor, and these eventually led him to a family living in the village of Gourna, near the Valley of the Kings: the three Abd el-Rassul brothers. One finally admitted that the three had been dealing in stolen burial goods and on 5 July 1881 he revealed the whereabouts of the cache, high up in a rock face.

Luigi Mayer's, *Egyptian antiquities in the hallway of a country house in Bulaq,* (above) in *Views in Egypt,* 1801–4. Below: photograph of the mummy of Ramesses II.

Maspero and his fellow archaeologists realized that the former masters of Egypt could not be treated in the same way as their obscure subjects and the entire contents of the Deir el-Bahari cache were transported by river to the museum at Bulaq, in the suburbs of Cairo. On both banks of the Nile, Maspero writes, 'dishevelled peasant women followed the boat howling like animals and the men fired shots in the way that they do at a funeral'. In Cairo they nevertheless had to pay duty on the mummies, which were classified as, of all things, dried fish.

In 1898 the French archaeologist Victor Loret (1859–1946) finds the tomb of Amenophis II in the Valley of the Kings. The pharaoh is still in his coffin

This was the first time that a royal tomb had been found complete with its occupant. Buried with the pharaoh was his bow, which he alone was entitled to draw. The mummies of eight other pharaohs from the New Kingdom were discovered in a side-chamber of the tomb. These were taken to Cairo; Amenophis (1421–1401 BC) remained where he was. His peace was short lived, however. Word soon got round that there were still treasures in the tomb and, despite the presence of an armed guard, it was looted and the pharaoh's body torn to pieces. From the ensuing enquiry it appeared that the guards themselves may have had some hand in the affair.

The archaeological exploration of tombs and burial sites became a regular and more systematic operation than hitherto. At the beginning of the 20th century the large burial chambers at Abydos, in the Valley of the

Howard Carter opening one of the four gilded wood shrines, the innermost of which housed the quartzite sarcophagus containing the wooden coffins of Tutankhamun (above). Opposite: bust of Tutankhamun found in the antechamber to his tomb. The figure, which is made of wood covered with painted plaster, has a fairly lifelike expression and wears the headdress associated with the god Amun. What function it served is not known.

The funerary mask of Prince Khaemuset, from the time of Ramesses II, found at Saqqara (left).

Kings, at Saqqara and in Nubia were all excavated, as were many less important sites. These excavations brought to light abundant artifacts and human or animal remains.

At around this time the first anthropological studies were undertaken, primarily on skeletons. X-raying, used on mummies from 1896 onwards, failed to produce any significant results until the 1930s. Unfortunately, unless they belonged to kings or important court officials, mummies were still not always studied with the attention they deserved.

For years the young English artist and Egyptologist Howard Carter (1874–1939) explores the Valley of the Kings, convinced that, contrary to popular opinion, there are still secrets to be uncovered

In November 1922 Carter entered the virtually intact tomb of Tutankhamun (1333–1323 BC), an obscure pharaoh of the end of the 18th Dynasty. It was the first time that an archaeologist had ever discovered a royal tomb with almost all its burial goods in place. These were for the most part of the highest quality, and it would take six years to remove them all from the chamber. Given the astonishing wealth lavished on a young king who reigned briefly during a period of great political upheaval, we can only guess what riches the tomb of a king as powerful as Ramesses II might have contained.

'A marvellous journey worthy of the Thousand and One Nights'

On 17 March 1939, after a decade of excavation at Tanis, the French archaeologist Pierre Montet

(1885–1966) discovered the tomb of Sheshonq I (945–924 BC), a pharaoh from the 22nd Dynasty, the Shishak of the Bible. Tanis, a vast site in the eastern Delta, had been a city of great importance at the end of the New Kingdom. Sheshonq's burial chamber was situated within the precinct of the temple of Amun.

The sarcophagi and funerary goods of a number of other pharaohs were subsequently uncovered, notably those of Psusennes I (21st Dynasty, 1040–992 BC). The Tanis excavations were certainly as important as the discovery of Tutankhamun's tomb, but the significance of the find was obscured by the outbreak of the Second World War a few months later.

The Tanis tombs were the last royal tombs to be uncovered. Some three hundred kings ruled Egypt, but many of their tombs have never been found: about twenty-five burial chambers have been uncovered, along with a few dozen pyramids. Moreover, very few royal mummies have survived intact.

Other discoveries, though less spectacular, have provided Egyptologists with a mine of information

Excavations of other burial sites have continued under the auspices of the Egyptian Antiquities Service and a number of foreign archaeological missions. At Saqqara,

P ectoral ornament belonging to Sheshonq II (above left), depicting a scarab beetle, symbol of rebirth. Left: gold plaque used to conceal the abdominal opening through which Psusennes's vital organs were removed; right: the same pharaoh's gold sandals. All these objects, found at Tanis, were clearly designed for ceremonial purposes.

a large site (50 km by 3 km) known to house a number of very ancient tombs as well as some much later ones, recent excavations have uncovered tombs belonging to court officials of the New Kingdom period. Much more modest sites from a range of periods are currently being excavated in the Theban region (the Valley of the Queens), the oases of the western desert (Duch, Balat and Muzawaga), Middle Egypt (Antinoë), the Fayuum and the Delta, and many mummies have been uncovered in the course of these excavations. Numerous teams of botanists, anthropologists and radiologists provide back-up research at many sites. Thanks to their combined efforts it has been possible to produce much more systematic population studies.

Mummies, still wrapped in their bandages (above), excavated from the Graeco-Roman necropolis at Antinoë at the beginning of this century. These early excavations were carried out in a random fashion, the mummies being removed to different locations, and in some cases destroyed. As a result, no systematic overview of the mummies was ever undertaken.

The practice of mummification dates back to the 3rd Dynasty, to around 2600 BC, but it was only in the 21st Dynasty, in c. 1000 BC, that the technique was perfected. It took centuries of experiment, and repeated failures, before the ancient Egyptians mastered the complex art of preserving in their dead the appearance of the living.

CHAPTER 2
IMPROVING TECHNIQUES

A detail from the Hildesheim sarcophagus (between 600 and 300 BC), contains a rare depiction of the mummification process (left). In Predynastic Egypt (before 3000 BC) bodies were buried either in the sand or in a pot, as here (right).

Approximately six thousand years ago, during the Predynastic Period, prior to the unification of Upper and Lower Egypt, the dead were buried in simple graves dug in the desert sands. The sand had a desiccating and therefore preservative effect on the body thus buried. The desire to afford better protection for the dead, however, coupled with technological advances led to the construction of more elaborate tombs in the course of the 1st Dynasty (2920–2770 BC).

The protection of the body was not the only consideration: at least for kings and major court officials, funerary rites were another factor influencing burial customs. An important tomb required a chapel, where offerings could be left, and also chambers for housing the burial goods. In this type of tomb, known as a mastaba, the body was placed in a chamber at the bottom of a shaft. In the simpler style of tomb the body was buried in a wooden or basketwork coffin inside a walled grave. In either case, deprived of the preservative effect of the sand, the body soon rotted: the very improvements intended to contribute to its preservation produced, in fact, the opposite effect. A different solution had to be found.

The mummy of a man, known as 'Ginger', who died in c. 3200 BC, was found at Gebelein, in the desert. Ginger, who is now conserved in the British Museum in London, is a good example of natural mummification. The discovery of bodies preserved in this way by the sand may have inspired in the ancient Egyptians the idea of life after death and led them to devise techniques for preserving the body. From this period onwards they placed vessels containing offerings, and everyday objects, in the vicinity of their dead.

The first tentative experiments

One idea was to wrap the body in cloth in order to protect it from the atmosphere. Coating the cloth in resin – so that it would stiffen and hold the body's original shape – also enhanced the preservative effect.

At the end of the 3rd Dynasty (2649–2575 BC) the embalmers began removing the body's abdominal organs – a fact that is indirectly confirmed by the appearance of Canopic jars, the stone vessels designed to hold these organs. They also discovered the dehydrating effect of natron, a naturally-occurring compound of sodium carbonate and sodium chloride, on human and animal tissue. The viscera of Queen Hetepheres, wife of Snofru, first king of the 4th Dynasty and father of Cheops, have been found coated in natron in an alabaster box divided into four compartments.

Results, nevertheless, remain unimpressive for mummies from the Old Kingdom (2575–2134 BC). The bandaging process, on the other hand, became fairly sophisticated, with bandages being arranged to imitate the hang of everyday clothes. The person's facial features were painted on to the shroud and in certain cases a further refinement was introduced by coating the cloth with a layer of plaster so as to preserve the angles and curves of the body (a technique that was soon abandoned).

Canopic jars with, beneath them, the human remains they contained (above). Champollion, who was the first to discover the use of Canopic jars, noted: 'Fibrous tissue ... Animal smell/Object impregnated and covered in a thick layer of balm/Found at the bottom of the vase/Just wrapped in cloth .../ Liver and brain or cerebellum.' Below: a mummy in the Egyptian Museum, Turin.

Dehydration using natron and removal of the abdominal organs gradually become widespread practices

Both the desiccation of the body and the removal of internal organs appear to have been widespread practices during the Middle Kingdom (2040–1640 BC) and results improved. Numerous mummies from this period have survived intact. That of Wah, an official under Mentuhotep III (11th Dynasty), was wrapped in a vast quantity of material – 375 sq. m in total. Where cheap preparations were required, the embalmers made do with sand – the treatment almost certainly reserved for Mentuhotep's soldiers, whose bodies were discovered at Deir el-Bahari.

The oldest known embalming instruments and materials,

Instruments used for mummification and funeral rites (above). Top: knife used to make the abdominal incision; middle left: adze, which had the purely symbolic function of breathing life into the corpse's mouth during the ritual known as the 'Opening of the Mouth'; right: vessel used to introduce the resin into the skull.

used for a person by the name of Ipy, date from this period. It appears that any remnants that may have been produced by the embalming process were placed near the body, since they were thought to contain fragments of the deceased person.

Important advances were made during the New Kingdom with the arrival of the 18th Dynasty, and numerous mummies have survived from that period, many of them in very good condition. Much of what we know about mummification at this date comes from the study of royal mummies, which invariably received particularly careful treatment due to their status.

Embalming 'according to the best of ways'

The Greek historian Herodotus wrote his nine-volume *History*, a narrative account of the wars between Greece and Persia, more than 2400 years ago. It also contains much incidental information gathered in the course of the

Seti I (1306–1290 BC) as found in his tomb at Deir el-Bahari, his arms crossed over his chest 'Osiris' fashion (above). His mummy is extremely well preserved and is a testimony to the embalming skills of the New Kingdom. The storage box for Canopic jars (far left) dates from the same period and is decorated with a statue of Anubis, the jackal-headed god who led the dead to judgment, and scenes of the dead person at prayer. Canopic jars were placed under the protection of the four sons of Horus, seen here on the lids of these jars (left). They are (left to right): Imsety, Hapy, Duamutef and Qebehsenuef, guardians of the liver, lungs, stomach and intestines.

author's travels, including an essentially accurate description of the mummification process (as confirmed by modern experts). Further details are found in the account of Diodorus Siculus, a Greek writing in the mid-1st century BC.

Two or three days after a person died, the body was delivered to the embalmers who immediately extracted the viscera through an incision made below the left ribs; they removed the liver, stomach, intestines and finally the lungs. The heart was regarded as the seat of consciousness and feeling (equivalent of the brain today). It was therefore essential that it was not separated from the body, and was generally left in place. The kidneys, spleen, bladder and female reproductive organs did not receive any special treatment on the whole.

The removal of the brain was a New Kingdom innovation. Using a bronze rod which was inserted into the left nostril, the embalmer smashed the ethmoid bone (located at the root of the nose and separating it from the cranium) and removed the brain through the aperture. Molten resin was then generally injected into the cranial cavity, and the resin (the precise composition of which is not known) solidified on contact with the skull. Alternatively sawdust or cloth was packed in.

The body was sewn up again, cleaned and then covered in natron in order to dehydrate it. The natron was applied in solid form, rather than in solution as the term 'natron bath' is often taken to imply. This operation according to Herodotus required no less than seventy days, although this seems in fact to have been the time needed for the entire mummification process. The body was next washed in Nile water and anointed with various unguents to make it smooth and 'sweet smelling'. Finally, it was laid on a funeral bed, which took the shape of a lion, prior to being dressed.

Engraving (above) of a late mummy (the inscription is in Greek) in Frédéric Cailliaud's *Voyage à Méroé* (of 1826–7). The incision is clearly visible, as it also is in this earlier mummy (below).

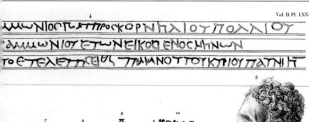

This anthropoid coffin of richly-decorated wood (below) belonged to a priestess living in the 21st Dynasty (1070–945 BC). Her name and religious status are inscribed on the lid. Her mummy, carefully shrouded and bandaged, was still in place when the coffin was found. The stereotypical features painted on the mask are not intended as a portrait.

'Here come plants sprung from the earth, flax and restoratives. They come to you in the form of a precious shroud; they preserve you in the form of bandages; they make you grow larger in the form of linen …'
(Embalming ritual)

The bandaging process was governed by a strict ritual specified in sacred books. At each step the officiating priest recited ritual formulas drawn from the texts.

The process began with the fingers, which were bandaged individually. Then came the limbs, which were also bandaged separately before being wrapped in large shrouds held in place by broader strips of cloth. The arms either rested alongside the body or were crossed over the chest in what was known as the 'Osiris' pose. The head came last.

The cloth was sometimes daubed with resin, and amulets were placed between the various layers. As many as 143 amulets and other small objects were found on the mummy of Tutankhamun and in the Graeco-Roman Period (332 BC – AD 395) the mummy of an ordinary man or woman still concealed forty or so.

The body was now fully protected and the *Book of the Dead* reads: 'Hail, Father Osiris! I shall possess my body for ever; I shall not be corrupted; I shall not disintegrate; nor will I fall prey to worms. I exist. I am alive. I am strong. I have awoken and am at peace. There is no destruction in my organs, or in my eyes; my head has not been removed from my neck … my body is permanent; it will not perish; it will not be destroyed in this eternal land.' The mummy was then placed in a coffin and returned to the family of the deceased in readiness for the funeral rites.

The mummy of a baby (above), found in its mother's coffin, has several strings of glass beads, either for decoration or for protection. Amulets (left), were often placed in the wrappings for protection. The *djed* pillar (second left) was a symbol of stability; the *ankh* or looped cross (second from right) gave the breath of life, and the *udjat* eye (centre top) had protective powers. Right: the heart-shaped amulet *ib* and the two-feathers.

'For those who desire the middle way and wish to avoid great cost'

The processes described above were very expensive, but according to Herodotus there also existed two other methods of embalming which were quicker and therefore cost less. The first of these involved injecting an oil into the anus to

dissolve the viscera prior to coating the body in natron. In the case of the second, and cheapest, method the body was simply washed and desiccated using natron. Mummies in this category have upon examination revealed remnants of the viscera in various stages of decomposition.

The bandaging technique might also vary. In some cases the fingers were not bandaged separately, and the cloth, which represented the biggest expense, might be of inferior quality, or recycled household linen, rather than specially made, as it was for first-rate embalming.

During the 21st Dynasty attempts are made to improve presentation

Clay, sawdust or pads of cloth were inserted under the skin in order to enhance the contours of face and body. Artificial eyes made of glass or wood, or linen pads, were sometimes placed in the eye sockets. These attempts met

This badly damaged mummy (above), found at Antinoë, was claimed by its excavator to be that of Thaïs, the heroine of a novel by Anatole France. Thaïs was a prostitute in Alexandria who was converted by the monk she set out to seduce and ended her days as a penitent in the desert.

The dead person, in the company of his wife and relatives, is carried to his resting place on a sleigh drawn by oxen. A scene from the Ani papyrus (19th Dynasty).

with varying degrees of success, and some mummies still display the unfortunate results of being overstuffed.

Mummification became a widespread practice from roughly 1000 BC onwards, which led to an increasing simplification of technique. In this sense it is possible to speak of a decline, although it was only a relative decline and there is evidence that fine workmanship did continue.

The practice of mummification persisted after the arrival of the Greeks (332 BC) and, later, the Romans (after 30 BC) and was even adopted by many foreigners living in Egypt. The work was often still of very high quality, though it is true that numerous mummies dating from this period are poorly preserved – a reflection of sloppy workmanship and probably also constraints on costs. Some are just bags of bones, with limbs dislocated and supported with palm branches. In other cases limbs have disappeared altogether. And yet other mummies from the period demonstrate the most careful attention to detail, with an emphasis on highly elaborate bandaging techniques involving geometric designs and plaster decorations. It seems that at this time more effort went into the bandaging than the embalming process. Also in the Graeco-Roman period the funeral mask was replaced by a portrait painted on a wooden panel, which was then inserted into the wrappings.

In Graeco-Roman Egypt the funeral mask was replaced by a portrait painted on wood (left). Some of the more elaborate mummies have leaves of electrum (an alloy of gold and silver) applied to their skin. The 'gilding' of the face (as above) or the limbs conferred a divine character on the recipient, since gold was regarded as the 'flesh of the gods'. Highly elaborate wrapping techniques, especially involving diamond designs (left), were adopted for the wealthy. Often a painted shroud, as in the case of this one for a child (near right), replaced both sarcophagus and cartonnage. The 'embroideress' of Antinoë (far right) was not bandaged at all, but simply wrapped in patterned tunics and shawls – a custom which broke with the pharaonic tradition.

Christian mummies

The spread of Christianity in Egypt from the 3rd and especially the 4th century AD did not put a stop to mummification. There is no evidence of any Church prohibition and, indeed, the preservation of the body might well be regarded as compatible with the Christian belief in resurrection.

The few Christian mummies that have been studied reveal only minor variations from the classical treatment. It did become customary to bury the dead in everyday clothes or in ceremonial vestments rather than wrapping the corpse in bandages.

The Pure Place

The first mummies were treated in a tent or some other light structure, located near the necropolis. This housed the embalming table on which the mummy was disembowelled. In the Late Period (after 712 BC), as more and more mummies required treatment, these temporary workshops were replaced by permanent ones made of brick, which were often quite large. The ancient Egyptians called the embalming house *wabt*, the Pure Place, or *per nefer*, the Beautiful House – a reminder that the object of mummification was to purify and deify the dead person, regarded as an incarnation of Osiris.

The embalmers were organized into a strict hierarchy. The most important positions were the 'Controller of the Mysteries', 'God's Seal Bearer' and the 'Lector Priest'. They were responsible for the religious aspects of the proceedings and the first is often shown wearing the jackal-headed mask of Anubis, who was the god of mummification. They consulted the sacred texts for the correct procedure, recited the ritual formulas and supervised the work of a team of subordinate technicians, each of whom had his specialist task at each stage. During the Late Period the organization of this team is fairly well known.

A detail from a sarcophagus (left) showing the embalmer, wearing the mask of the jackal-headed god Anubis, bending over the mummy, which lies on a bed shaped like a lion. One of the few Anubis masks that have survived (above) is in painted terracotta, with two eye-holes.

The last stage of the earthly journey. A Ptolemaic papyrus showing a mummy on its way to the burial ground. The mummy is enclosed in a type of chest, which is carried on a barque, itself carried on a wheeled chariot hauled by a team of men – an innovation introduced at the end of the pharaonic era. The group is led by a priest carrying a censer.

The line where the body was to be cut was marked by a priest called a 'scribe'. Then the *paraschistes*, or 'ripper-up', made the incision for the removal of the viscera. He used a knife made either of flint or of obsidian, a naturally-occurring volcanic glass which had to be imported into Egypt. The job of the *taricheutes*, the embalmer, was to desiccate the body using natron, while other specialists were responsible for its transportation and burial. The funeral service and, later on, the ceremony during which offerings were made, were conducted by designated priests.

All of the various artisans belonged to a guild and held an office which he could either sell or pass on to descendants or to a third party. Each of them had exclusive rights over a section of the population of a village or town, with the result that the necropolises were divided into sectors and conflicts over the rights to a body frequently ensued.

The men who worked at the Pure Place were paid in kind – and, during the Late Period, also in money – by the family of the deceased. Despite the importance of their role, they probably did not enjoy a high status in the community. They appear to have been obliged to live outside the town, no doubt on account of the peculiar nature of their activities.

Model of a funeral barque, found in a Middle Kingdom tomb. Such barques serve as a reminder that the dead did indeed have to make a river crossing in order to reach their final resting place, since the burial grounds were located in the desert, on the western bank of the Nile.

'**Y**ou will be like Re, rising and setting through all eternity.' The ancient Egyptians regarded death as a transition to another life and mummification as the necessary preparation for entry into the eternal abode.

CHAPTER 3

TOWARDS IMMORTALITY

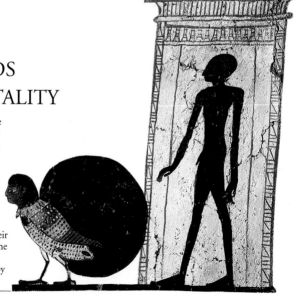

Hovering over the blackened body of a mummy, the *Ba*, or bird-soul (with a human head), awaits its magical reunion with the body (left); illustration from the *Book of the Dead*. Right: detail from Arinefer's tomb at Deir el-Medina showing the dead person leaving the tomb, preceded by his *Ba*.

To the ancient Egyptians every living creature was made up of a material structure, the body, to which were attached immaterial elements, including the *Ba*, the equivalent of the soul, or the personality, and the *Ka*, the life force. In death these different elements became separated.

An amulet in the shape of two frogs (left). The frog, a creature of the swamp (primordial waters), was a symbol of eternal life.

'Your legs will carry you to the eternal abode and your hands will carry for you as far as the place of infinite duration' (Embalming ritual)

In order to enter its second life, the body had to be reunited with the spiritual elements which had previously animated it. In other words it had to be preserved, and at every step of the mummification process magic formulas reassured the dead person that his body was still intact. The destruction of the body was a very serious matter, signifying, as it did, the impossibility of resurrection. To guard against such an evil, from the Old Kingdom onwards replicas of the dead person – either statues or 'reserve heads', as they were known – were placed in the tombs of kings and noblemen and served as magical replacements of a destroyed or damaged body.

Given the importance accorded to burial practices and monuments, one might be forgiven for assuming that the ancient Egyptians set little store by life itself. In fact they regarded it as the most precious of all gifts. As one New Kingdom inscription reads, 'Your happiness weighs more heavily than the life to come'.

Death was viewed both as a simple transition from one life to the next and as a termination, the point of entry to 'the place from

Papyrus (right) from the tomb of Tuthmosis III showing (middle panel) the king as the sun god travelling across the sky, the 'celestial ocean', in the solar barque. Baboons (upper panel), the animals associated with Thoth, god of learning, are shown adoring the sun, with funerary divinities at prayer. The rising sun (lower panel) is depicted as a scarab beetle in its barque.

which one never returns'. In the Old Kingdom life after death was still pictured in rather nebulous terms, with the king alone enjoying a privileged destiny. According to the stellar myth he went to join the 'fixed' (circumpolar) stars and live with the gods, with whom he became identified. In the solar myth he accompanied the sun in its course across the 'celestial ocean' and participated in its daily rebirth. As far as ordinary men and women were concerned (though we have very little information) life after death probably consisted of a straightforward continuation of life on earth.

During the troubled 1st Intermediate Period (2134–2040 BC) provincial governors declared

Funerary statues, like these (left), and reserve heads, like the one pictured above, served as magical replacements if the mummy was damaged. The name of the deceased was inscribed on the statue, since a name was thought to be imbued with life once it was written down.

themselves equal in status to the king, and the ruling class, which was becoming increasingly powerful, laid claim to royal prerogatives in terms of immortality. Mummification and the religious formulas designed to ensure such immortality, originally the preserve of royalty, became available to increasing numbers of people. Many sought to be buried near Osiris' principal tomb, at Abydos, where the kings of the first dynasties had built themselves cenotaphs. Or, failing this, they had a stele erected there so that they could still continue to enjoy the protection of the god of the dead.

'I am complete. I am justified. I am youthful. For, in truth, I am Osiris, Lord of all Eternity' *Book of the Dead*

Ideas about what the afterlife entailed crystallized during the New Kingdom. The world of the dead was viewed as a subterranean kingdom which was ruled over by Osiris, as both king – his own experience of death and resurrection qualified him for the title god of the dead – and the embodiment of the life force.

In the New Kingdom ordinary people adopted royal myths. On the coffin of a woman named Taneteret the solar barque is preceded by Anubis.

A dead man with his wife in the afterlife. This seems to be a continuation of earthly delights, with a table of offerings and a game of senet set in front of them.

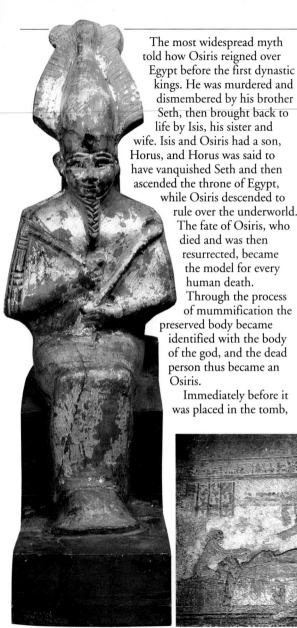

The most widespread myth told how Osiris reigned over Egypt before the first dynastic kings. He was murdered and dismembered by his brother Seth, then brought back to life by Isis, his sister and wife. Isis and Osiris had a son, Horus, and Horus was said to have vanquished Seth and then ascended the throne of Egypt, while Osiris descended to rule over the underworld. The fate of Osiris, who died and was then resurrected, became the model for every human death.

Through the process of mummification the preserved body became identified with the body of the god, and the dead person thus became an Osiris.

Immediately before it was placed in the tomb,

A statuette of Osiris made of gilded schist (left), showing him in all his majesty. He is equipped with his traditional attributes – wearing a shroud and the crown of Atef, and holding the royal flail and crook. He has his arms crossed over his chest in a gesture frequently imitated by the embalmers.

A wall painting in the temple of Dendera showing Osiris on his funeral bed on the point of impregnating Isis, who hovers over him in the form of a bird. The product of this union was Horus, the royal protector (a living king was an incarnation of Horus, a dead king an incarnation of Osiris). The bird on the right represents Nephthys, Isis' sister.

the mummified body, already resting in its coffin, was raised up in front of the door to the tomb where it was given the 'breath of life' by means of a ritual known as the 'Opening of the Mouth' ceremony. Magically brought back to life, the mummy was then presented with various offerings of food and deposited in the tomb, which henceforth would be its 'dwelling place for millions of years'.

The second life, which began at burial, is represented in great detail by New Kingdom illustrators and their successors. Anubis, keeper of the kingdom of the dead, led the dead person to receive judgment in the presence of Osiris, revealed now in all his glory. During judgment the dead person was obliged to recite the double 'negative confession', declaring himself innocent of a whole series of crimes, both general and specific, against the gods and against humanity, proclaiming, among other things:

'I have not added to the weight of the scales.
I have not carried away the milk from the mouths of children.
I have not driven away the cattle which were upon their pastures.'

A priest performing the 'Opening of the Mouth' (above). The door of the tomb opens on to stairs leading to the vault, where the bird-soul of the dead man hovers. Below: the 'Weighing of the Heart' ceremony.

Next came the 'Weighing of the Heart', or psychostasia. The heart, on one side of the balance, should be as light as a feather (symbol of Maat, the embodiment of truth and justice), but if it proved too heavy – if, in other words, the dead person's crimes outweighed his good deeds – Ammit the Gobbler was waiting open-mouthed to consume and consign him to a second, lasting, death. Thoth, the god of wisdom and knowledge, recorded the result of the weighing process in the presence of Osiris and other attendant gods.

The dead person is now 'justified' and free to undertake the journey through the underworld

As a guide on the journey through the underworld the dead person had a copy of the *Book of the Dead* on a roll of papyrus which was placed inside the coffin, on the mummy itself, or in a box serving as the pedestal to a statue of Osiris. This papyrus was illustrated with scenes constituting a sort of map of the afterlife. This was a world peopled with strange and terrifying creatures, criss-crossed with canals, lakes, roads and gates guarded by knife-wielding spirits. The book also contained magic formulas instructing the dead person on how to overcome the obstacles that lay ahead and how to find the kingdom of the blessed.

An illustration from the Hunefer *Book of the Dead* (above), showing the dead person (left) being led to judgment by Anubis and (right) standing before Osiris; in the centre: the 'Weighing of the Heart' ceremony. Below: Opet, the hippopotamus goddess, and Hathor, the cow goddess, emerging from the mountain of the West; illustration from the Ani *Book of the Dead.*

Journey to the kingdom of the dead

Once in the underworld the dead person was confronted with a series of tests. The magic formulas contained in what the Egyptians called the *Book of the Entry into the Light*, or *Book of the Dead*, were designed to help in any situation that might be encountered. This illustration from the *Book of the Dead* shows the dead man (left) lying on his funeral bed and (right) incarnated as Osiris in the company of Anubis and falcon-headed Horus, who place their arms around him in a gesture of protection. The face and headdress are those traditionally attributed to Osiris, and the body of the dead man is represented as the *djed* pillar, symbol of strength and stability. Note how the serpent beneath the bed is transfixed with knives and thereby rendered powerless. The book's formula for banishing the serpent runs: 'Be gone! Go and drown yourself in the lake of the Abyss, where your father commanded that you should perish! I am Re, before whom men tremble. Be gone, rebel, lest you feel his knives of light!'

The mere presence of this book alongside the mummy was sufficient to ensure its survival in the afterlife. Other funerary books of a more theological nature – the *Book of Gates*, the *Book of Caverns* and the *Book of Douat* [the kingdom of the dead] *and What It Contains* – were reserved for royal tombs and served merely as decoration.

The *Book of the Dead* first appeared in the New Kingdom and brought together a number of ancient traditions, some of which go back, via the Coffin Texts inscribed on the walls of Middle Kingdom sarcophagi,

'I have acquired this field … Here I eat and drink and feast; here I plough and I harvest', *Book of the Dead*. Below: illustration from the Ani *Book of the Dead* depicting life in the other world.

to the Pyramid Texts. These were engraved on the walls of the mortuary chambers in the royal pyramids from the 5th Dynasty (2465–2323 BC) onwards. Originally reserved for the king, in a modified form they were gradually adopted for universal use.

Animals

Many tombs housed animal as well as human occupants. A baboon was discovered, for example, in the tomb of a Theban priestess of the 21st Dynasty, and more modest

A richly-decorated sarcophagus for a falcon (left) is topped by a statue of the bird wearing the plumed crown of Horus. Other sarcophagi might be carved in the shape of the animal they housed. Opposite: two falcon mummies, the one on the right wearing a mask and as intricately wrapped as any human mummy, the one on the left altogether more simple.

tombs housed dogs, cats and birds –
probably household pets which their
owners wished to keep with them in the
afterlife. Some animals even had their
own coffin: the favourite cat of
Prince Tuthmosis, eldest son of
Amenophis III, was buried in a
limestone sarcophagus
(discovered at Memphis) bearing
the inscription 'Osiris Ta-miat
the Justified One'.

The ancient Egyptians would
have seen nothing odd about
mummifying animals: they made
no essential distinction between
humans and animals and the lives of
both were closely interwoven in
ancient Egypt.

Gods could take animal as well as human form

Animal worship was a permanent
feature of Egyptian civilization. Gods
might assume different forms at
different periods in history, but their
essential attributes remained the same. Thus, the falcon
Horus, an ancient incarnation of royal power, was
sometimes represented as the bird itself and sometimes
as a man with a bird's head. The Apis Bull, at Memphis,
and the Ram of Mendes and that of Elephantine, on the
other hand, retained their animal form throughout the
course of ancient Egyptian civilization.

These animals were regarded as living gods and
were therefore destined for immortality through
mummification. They were unique. There was only one
Apis Bull, recognizable by distinctive markings on his
hide. He had his own temple where he was worshipped
and a sacred living enclosure where his followers came
to see him. When he died he was mummified and the
funeral rites resembled those performed at human
burials. His remains were deposited in a massive granite
sarcophagus, placed originally in an individual tomb

and then, later on, in a huge collective vault – the famous Serapeum at Saqqara. The necropolis dedicated to the Sacred Cows, the Mothers of Apis, was located nearby.

Worship and funerary rites were similar in the case of the Mnevis Bull at Heliopolis, the Buchis Bull at Armant and the Ram of Mendes and the Ram of Elephantine, also regarded as living gods. The crocodile god Sobek was worshipped in the Fayuum and at Kom Ombo, and Sobek temples housed sacred crocodiles, one of which may have been regarded as the incarnation of the god himself. Herodotus describes how the people of Thebes and the Fayuum each had their own tame crocodile, which they fed and looked after. The crocodile wore earrings and bracelets on its front legs, and was given sacred food. Strabo, writing four centuries later, adds: 'The sacred crocodile is fed in a lake of its own; the priests know how to tame it and they call it Soukos [Sobek].'

Ibises were mummified by the thousands. Left: a watercolour of a mummified ibis in the *Description of Egypt*, with, beside it, a ceramic pot containing several ibises.

A detail from a stele in the Buchis necropolis showing the Buchis Bull, incarnation of the god Monthu, receiving offerings from Ptolemy V Epiphanes. An inscription states that the bull died aged thirteen years, ten months and twenty-eight days.

Certain animals were associated with particular gods – for example, the cat with Bastet and the ibis and the baboon with Thoth

The hundreds of thousands, sometimes millions, of ibis and cat mummies discovered in the necropolises were apparently offerings bought specially by pilgrims to be mummified and presented to their respective gods. The temple to the goddess Bastet at Bubastis and that of the god Thoth at Hermopolis reared sacred cats and ibises, it seems, expressly for sacrificial purposes – a practice which became very widespread from the first millennium BC. Other animals were also treated in the same way.

A rather different case is presented by the mummy of a frog found in a tomb in the village of Duch (in the Kharga oasis), resting between the thighs of a castrated and mummified adult male. According to one version of the Osirian myth, when Osiris was dismembered his penis was thrown into the Nile and devoured by fish. The Duch mummy – whose arms are crossed in the traditional Osirian position – appears to have been modelled on this myth. The presence of the frog, which is a symbol of rebirth, affirms the belief in the future life of the dead man.

Three stages in the unwrapping of the mummy of a ram from the town of Elephantine, whose principal deity was the ram-god Khnum.

A menagerie of sacrificial victims

The embalmers of ancient Egypt mummified a whole range of animals, both household and sacred. Clockwise, from opposite above left: a monkey with a crowned human head; two ducks (a regular source of food, also used in offerings to the dead); crocodile eggs; three cats; a dog; crocodile remains and mummy; a fish. Crocodiles come especially from Kom Ombo and the Fayuum. They were often wrapped with great care, as here; several animals of varying sizes might be wrapped together, in various states of preservation, with the occasional inclusion of eggs.

'**H**ow well equipped you are, inhabitant of the other world!' To facilitate life in the other world, the ancient Egyptians furnished their dead with offerings, which could sometimes be of considerable value. The direct consequence of this – the pillaging of tombs – was to become a national pastime, and was a fate that few tombs, however simple, escaped.

CHAPTER 4

FROM ETERNAL LIFE
TO HARSH REALITY

Eyes painted on a Middle Kingdom coffin allowed the dead still to see. Opposite: the King's Chamber in the Great Pyramid, painted by Luigi Mayer in the early 19th century. The granite sarcophagus of the pharaoh Cheops was found empty.

So impressive are the funerary monuments and their contents that one is forced to conclude that the ancient Egyptians devoted the major part of their resources to setting up their 'eternal home'. The royal tombs provide the most obvious illustration of this. Incredible energy and considerable financial resources went into the construction of the pyramids and the burial vaults in the Valley of the Kings, not to mention the funerary temples, such as Chephren's Valley Temple, and the Ramesseum and Medinet Habu of Ramesses II and III respectively. The sums spent on constructing tombs for the average man and woman were also proportionally large.

Sennedjem's tomb at Deir el-Medina (below) is in typical New Kingdom style, with its underground vaults and complex superstructures. Note the funerary chapel surmounted by a small pyramid, the temple-façade gateway and the deep shaft, equipped with handholds, leading to the underground chambers.

Tomb architecture varies little over the centuries, with few basic types

Tomb types depended on local topography and the financial resources of the owner. Simple burials in graves are found in every period, but the more complex tombs underwent a number of changes. Mastabas (low, rectangular buildings) were built during the Old and the Middle Kingdom, and rock-cut tombs first appeared at the end of the Old Kingdom. Tombs with a pyramidal superstructure – the most sophisticated of which are the royal pyramids of the Old Kingdom (such as those of the pharaohs Cheops, Chephren

Two different types of royal tomb: (opposite) Chephren's pyramid (4th Dynasty), painted by Luigi Mayer; (left) Queen Merneith's mastaba (1st Dynasty) at Saqqara.

and Mykerinus) – were still being built as private tombs during the New Kingdom, albeit on a much more modest scale. The same style was adopted at Meroë in Upper Nubia. One final innovation was a chapel added to the tomb, first built in the New Kingdom.

The tomb is the dead person's new habitat, a world governed by magic, where existence continues, but in a different way

The environment of everyday life simply had to be represented in various ways for the dead person to continue to enjoy it. Traditional images show the deceased sitting in front of a table laden with food, and hunting and farming scenes may have a similar significance, though they may merely have been intended to evoke real life in general, rather than

Early 19th-century adventurers, including the Marseilles sculptor Jean-Jacques Rifaud, had no qualms about rifling coffins and valuable objects from the depths of burial chambers like this one at Gourna pictured in cross-section below. Rifaud, who spent forty years in Egypt, indicates on the drawing how he managed to manoeuvre the coffin up to the surface.

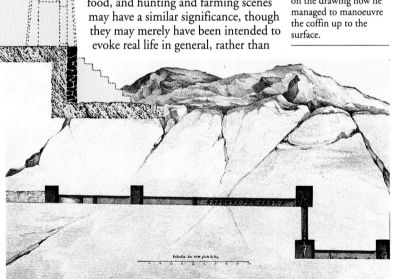

Echelle de 100 pieds du Roy

particular personal circumstances.

For the same reason the dead are always represented as young and in full possession of their faculties. This was particularly true in the case of the pharaohs – who began work on their tombs more or less as soon as they came to power, while they were in fact still relatively young. Models evoking various activities of daily life and models of houses – 'soul houses' – are frequently

Royal tombs, like that of Seti I at Thebes (above), were decorated with scenes of primarily religious inspiration. Scenes from everyday life tended to be reserved for the ordinary man and woman. This detail (left) from Nefertiabet's stele shows the dead woman seated in front of a table laden with bread.

encountered in the tombs of ordinary people from the Middle Kingdom and are a further reminder that the dead person continued to 'live' in a real sense.

'Offerings will be made and provisions of bread, beer, meat, poultry and incense will be given'
Book of the Dead

Offerings of food ensured the dead person's survival in the afterlife. The dead were also surrounded with objects from daily life – items of toiletry, clothes and fabric, pottery and stone vessels, arms – as in the case of Tutankhamun's weapons and Amenophis II's bow – tools relating to specific trades, such as writing materials, medical papyri, shuttles and spindles, and even toys.

Many of these objects would have been used by the dead person in real life; others had a merely ceremonial function. Tutankhamun's golden chariot, for example, had clearly never been used.

Food itself was mummified before being offered to the dead, as in the case of this basket of legs of lamb (above left) found in a tomb at Deir el-Bahari. Objects from daily life and models representing the lifestyle of the dead person were also placed in the tomb. Above: bronze mirror; below: model of a granary with cows.

The tomb also housed a range of ritual objects

Tomb contents included Canopic jars, designed to hold the mummified viscera, which were most widely used from the Middle Kingdom onwards, and ushabtis, mummiform figurines made of wood, stone or glazed frit (a kind of glass) which appeared at the same period. In the New Kingdom it became customary to place several hundred of these figurines near the coffin (one for each day of the year, with several 'overseers' to supervise them). As servants of the dead person, the ushabtis, or 'answerers', were supposed to undertake any tasks Osiris imposed on their owner in the life hereafter.

From the Middle Kingdom up until the Graeco-Roman Period nude female figures with exaggerated sexual characteristics were also placed in tombs belonging to both men and women. Described as 'concubines of the dead', they were in fact probably intended to facilitate sexual functioning in the afterlife.

❝ If any one of you is required to carry out a task in the other world, you will say "Present!" **❞** These words from the *Book of the Dead* were often inscribed on the ushabtis, or servants of the dead, as if to remind them of their role. These figurines vary in height from a few inches to a foot or more depending on the importance of their owner, and some, like this one (above right) belonging to Amenhotep, have their own miniature coffin in imitation of their owner's. Above left: chest containing Canopic jars belonging to Psametik, with the divine guardians of the viscera represented on the outside. Below: ushabtis belonging to Neferibre.

The mummy is encased in a series of protective containers, the elaborateness of which depends on the wealth of the dead person

The outermost container was either a stone sarcophagus – in the case of kings or important officials – or, more often, a wooden coffin. These were of either rectangular or anthropoid design. The decoration of the sarcophagus or coffin varied considerably over the centuries and included ritual texts (Coffin Texts in the Middle Kingdom), mythological scenes and biographical details, including the dead person's name, status and occupation.

The sarcophagus, or outermost coffin, originally contained a second, anthropoid coffin, which was usually made of wood. From the 22nd Dynasty (9th century BC) this second coffin was replaced by a

The first coffins were plain boxes made of wood or, in the case of pharaohs and important officials, stone, which sometimes had very thick sides (a stone sarcophagus could weigh several tons). Decoration, in the form of symbolic motifs and funerary texts, was introduced during the second half of the 2nd millennium BC and the name of the dead person was inscribed henceforth on the coffin lid. Anthropoid coffins – imitating, however

cartonnage, a container made of layers of linen or papyrus stiffened with glue or plaster and decorated with brightly coloured motifs frequently set off with gold. In the majority of cartonnages the lines of the body are barely suggested, while the facial features, framed by a heavy wig, are often highly expressive, if also often stereotyped. The pharaohs, and a few very wealthy individuals, had a third coffin, and the pharaohs also had a solid gold mask (those belonging to Psusennes and Tutankhamun have survived to this day). Finally came

crudely, the shape of their occupant – were also introduced. Menuf's sarcophagus (above), is of this type. Practically every sarcophagus and coffin had been opened before the archaeologists arrived on the scene.

The three richly decorated mummiform coffins belonging to a certain Tamutnefret, singer of Amun, plainly a woman of some standing. The lids are decorated with bands of text and funerary deities, including a winged goddess who envelops the dead woman in a gesture of protection. The funerary texts were a means of ensuring the dead person's continued existence in the afterlife. For instance, 'O my Lord, Osiris …' the royal scribe Unefer declaims, 'I was a man who was honoured by his father, praised by his mother and who behaved kindly towards his brothers. I have done nothing in this life to displease you. Give me incense for my eternal home and water for my tomb in the West.' Edfu, 'a good and kind woman … wife of the general, the king's brother', requests 'that her house be stable, that her possessions remain in their rightful place, that her children remain behind her on this earth, for ever'.

the mummy itself, wrapped in its layers of shrouds and bandages.

Only wealthier individuals could afford coffins and cartonnages. Many people were buried without either, but were simply wrapped in their shrouds and bandages. In the Late Period it was common for mummies merely to wear a gilded and painted plaster mask, and from the Graeco-Roman Period onwards a portrait painted in wax on wood was inserted inside the bandages wrapping the face. These are the so-called Fayuum portraits, from the place they were first found. Some mummies were wrapped in a large painted shroud, while the poorest folk were not mummified at all.

The painted shrouds of the Graeco-Roman Period were relatively stiff and were designed to cover the entire mummy once it had been bandaged. Left: shroud painted with a traditional scene from the *Book of the Dead*, showing the dead person, in classical costume, being presented to Osiris by Anubis.

During the Ptolemaic Dynasty (305–30 BC) cartonnages took the form of plaques, decorated with funerary motifs and protective symbols, attached directly to the shroud. This type of cartonnage always included a large floral collar (flowers were a symbol of renewal) and a 'foot box', as seen here on the mummy of Pachery.

The mummy was now fully prepared and equipped for the afterlife and ready to enter the tomb – its 'dwelling place for millions of years'. The dead still had to be protected from one thing, however, and that was the aggression and greed of their fellow men in the world of the living.

The dead who look at us

There was a new emphasis on realism in the presentation of mummies in Graeco-Roman Egypt, as if it had become important that the dead person should be easily recognized. Mummy portraits, such as these of a certain Ammonius and an unknown woman (opposite and left), were painted on wood or cloth with coloured wax or pigments mixed with a binding agent. The range of facial types, some very expressive, are a reflection of a highly cosmopolitan population. These portraits, which have no precedent in ancient Egypt, recall the Roman portraits found at Pompeii. Masks like the one above also date from this period and are quite different in style from traditional Egyptian masks.

From sarcophagi to shirts

Portraits were inserted in the bandages or the cartonnage, as in the case of Artemidorus (opposite, left), from the Graeco-Roman cemetery at Hawara (his name is written in Greek below the floral garland). Some mummies were covered with a net of coloured beads (opposite, right). The beads were made of faience (glazed earthenware) or simply painted on to the cartonnage. From the 4th century AD, it became customary to dress the dead in the clothes they had worn in life. Some of these are very well preserved and are of excellent workmanship. Left: clothing found in a tomb, from the *Description of Egypt*. Such innovations were a far cry from classical Egyptian coffins like that, below, belonging to a woman named Madja of the New Kingdom.

What happened to the mummies?

The looting of tombs became a widespread practice and increasingly sophisticated measures were adopted in an attempt to deter potential robbers. Vigorous competition between architects and robbers, each doing their best to outwit the other, continued from the first dynasties until the end of ancient Egyptian civilization.

The pyramids were lavishly equipped with magnificent funerary goods. To mount a direct assault on one of these was clearly no easy matter and in practice could only be done with the help of the guards. With the weakening of the central powers and the unrest that characterized the 1st Intermediate Period, however, the pyramids were no longer safe from intruders. Breaking into one could still not have been an easy task given the internal security arrangements – portcullises, false corridors and concealed openings, many of them sealed with blocks of stone – and yet every pyramid was broken into, and by the time the archaeologists arrived the funerary chambers were virtually stripped bare.

In the New Kingdom, for religious but also for security reasons, the pharaohs abandoned the pyramid – which was such an obvious focal point – in favour of more discreet underground burial chambers. Vast tombs

Luigi Mayer's painting of the *Interior view of the catacombs at Alexandria*, showing the square-sided pillars and Greek pediment typical of tombs in this region.

Tutankhamun's tomb is the only royal tomb to have remained substantially intact until modern times. It was broken into shortly after the king was buried, but luckily the intruders were disturbed. The photographs below and opposite show how the tomb looked when it was opened in 1922. Funerary goods were piled and scattered in disarray and one of the intruders had left his footprints on a chest (below).

Mummies excavated at the beginning of the 20th century (left). Above: a detail from the Abbott Papyrus, a record of a lawsuit brought against the looters of Ramesses II's tomb in the reign of Ramesses IX. Several arrests were made and the defendants admitted they had gone 'to steal from the tombs as [they were] accustomed to do', had opened the coffins of a king and a queen, removed the amulets, jewels and other precious objects and then set fire to the coffins.

were tunnelled in secret (at least initially) in the limestone cliffs overlooking the Valley of the Kings and the Valley of the Queens near Thebes, and the entrance to each tomb was generally concealed. But, despite the presence of a permanent guard whose job was to deter potential thieves, and despite the internal arrangements – the deep shafts, the dead ends, the enormously heavy granite sarcophagi, which were virtually impenetrable – these tombs were looted just like their predecessors.

The proof of this looting is contained in the fragmentary records of an action brought against looters in the reign of Ramesses IX (1131–1112 BC). Although nothing can be confirmed, there are hints in the robbers' statements which point to collusion at a high level, possibly even implicating the head of police in charge of the necropolis.

In the course of the following years increasing numbers of tombs were violated, notably those of Seti I and Ramesses II in the Valley of the Kings. Eventually, between 1070 and 945 BC, the high priests of Amun had the royal mummies of the 18th, 19th and 20th dynasties exhumed and reburied in secret caches, whose whereabouts were not discovered until the end of the 19th century. Inevitably most of these mummies had been stripped of valuables and had to be bandaged again for reburial.

In a Graeco-Roman tomb at Duch a letter dating from the last century concerning a supply of hay for a donkey was found – evidently left behind by a careless thief. In another case the intruder had been crushed when part of the roof of the tomb had caved in and his skeleton ended up keeping company with the mummies he had come to rob.

Emptying the tomb of Tutankhamun was a painstaking operation and some of the objects were restored on site. The entire collection is housed today in the Cairo Museum. Below: a photograph of the removal operations.

Tomb 20 in the necropolis at Duch (left), with its piles of bodies, furniture and funeral cloth, presents a similar scene to that in a watercolour by Sir John Gardner Wilkinson (right) of a peasant woman searching for antiquities in a tomb at Thebes (c. 1830).

Private tombs were also pillaged...

If it is not altogether surprising that royal tombs, known to conceal fabulous riches, were looted, one might have hoped that tombs belonging to ordinary men and women would be spared. On the whole, however, even the poorest private tombs were broken into, and had been since early antiquity. The enquiry conducted under Ramesses IX shows that all the civil tombs inspected had been violated.

It may seem curious that the ancient Egyptians, who are known to have been deeply religious, apparently had no qualms about depriving the dead of their means of survival in the other world. No doubt, for people struggling to survive, the temptation was simply too great, particularly during times of economic hardship, and, rather than professional thieves, the looters were often artisans and peasants working in the vicinity of the necropolises. The practice of pillaging tombs continued up until modern times, supplying the illegal trade in antiquities and destroying irreplaceable archaeological material. Thus archaeologists usually find tombs that have been stripped almost entirely bare.

... and ancient tombs reused

Reusing tombs was a fairly common practice, at least in the Late Period, and it is not unusual to find tombs built for a single occupant and his family piled high with mummies. Even the tombs of queens were subjected to this indignity, which usually led to the deterioration of the original occupants.

The pharaohs themselves set the precedent by 'recycling' sarcophagi, funerary goods and even tombs. A lion with a man's head from Tanis bears no fewer than three different royal inscriptions and Psusennes I (21st Dynasty) was buried in a sarcophagus that had originally housed an official of the 19th.

Mummies were unwrapped, stripped of their coverings and jewels and often removed from their supposed 'dwelling place for millions of years', and many of them failed to survive the ordeal.

In the 19th century Cairo was full of people such as these (below and opposite) selling figurines, amulets and jewelry to tourists. More valuable items were sold by established antiquaries, who had a network of contacts.

The birth of Egyptology produced a gradual revival of interest in mummies. Originally no more than objects of curiosity or raw material for pharmaceutical purposes, they became an important focus of scientific study. Archaeologists saved many from the hands of the pillagers and today, with the help of modern technology, they are engaged in trying to preserve this irreplaceable human material.

CHAPTER 5

UNDER THE EXPERT'S EYE

An X-ray of Ramesses II's nose. The mass of dark specks are grains of pepper, used as a preservative by the embalmers. The bone-like object above the nostril is in fact a plug of solidified resin designed to hold the pepper in place. Right: a mummy's arm, a watercolour from the *Description of Egypt*.

Throughout the 19th century the unwrapping of mummies was made the occasion for special ceremonies, to which a select public was invited; but these meetings were more like entertainment (of a rather morbid kind) than serious scientific enquiry. Things changed with the sensational discovery of the cache of royal mummies at Deir el-Bahari in July 1881. These illustrious mummies had to be conserved at all costs, and a new investigative approach was required (though, in the event, the unbandaging was carried out in a rather hasty and unceremonious fashion). The mummies were first housed in the museum in the Cairo suburb of Bulaq, then, in 1902, they were transferred to the newly-built Cairo Museum.

From this time on the unbandaging was often followed by a more or less complete autopsy. From this, information could be pieced together about the mummification process. Also any ailments or accidents suffered by the living person could be diagnosed from the mummified remains.

In 1895 the German scientist Wilhelm Konrad Röntgen discovered the X-ray and, on 8 November of the same year, he took an X-ray (the exposure time was half an hour) of his wife's hand. This discovery won Röntgen the first ever Nobel prize for physics in 1901. The great English archaeologist Sir William Matthew Flinders Petrie soon recognized the importance of the X-ray technique for Egyptology and took the first X-rays of mummies in 1896.

At last Egyptology has access to a harmless means of exploring mummified human remains: radiology

Radiographic equipment was not yet powerful enough, however, to do more than X-ray the body's extremities and when, in 1912, Sir Grafton Elliot Smith (1871–1937) published the first exhaustive description of the royal mummies conserved in Cairo, X-ray information formed only a small part of his findings.

Sarcophagi and Canopic jars (centre) at the museum at Bulaq, founded by Auguste Mariette (1821–81) in 1858. Mariette also discovered the Serapeum at Saqqara and founded the Egyptian Antiquities Service in an attempt to halt the systematic pillaging of ancient monuments. Opposite, left: Arthur Mace (1874–1928) cleaning an artifact in the tomb of Seti II at Luxor; right: Sir Gaston Maspero, Mariette's successor at Bulaq. His excavations included the pyramids of Giza and the temple at Luxor. Above: Sir William Matthew Flinders Petrie (seated, centre) with his wife and team of assistants. He was the outstanding figure in Egyptian archaeology at the turn of the century. An indefatigable explorer, he paid great attention to detail and was quite prepared to re-excavate sites already examined.

Application of the technique had encountered a major logistical difficulty: how to bring together, physically, the radiologist, the equipment and the mummy itself. Tuthmosis IV's mummy, for example, had to be taken by taxi to the hospital housing the first radiology unit in Cairo.

As X-ray techniques improved, interest in radiology grew. In 1913 scientists described the first lumbar-sacral abnormality observed in a mummy (this type of abnormality, widely encountered today, is responsible for sciatic pain and lumbago). In 1931 R.L. Moodie was able to record radiographic information for seventeen mummies, and by 1967 P.H.K. Gray had studied a total of 133 mummies conserved in various European museums, notably in Great Britain and the Netherlands.

Photographs of Tuthmosis II (right) and (left), possibly, Tuthmosis I. Despite an apparent family likeness, X-rays indicate that the latter's skeleton probably belongs in fact to a man much younger than the pharaoh is thought to have been.

J.E. Harris and K.R. Weeks begin a careful study of the royal mummies in the Cairo Museum

By identifying illnesses or physical characteristics, the researches of these scholars, published in 1973 and 1980, have authenticated such details as family links and confirmed some details of the ancient texts. For example, Seqenenre II, a pharaoh of the 16th century BC, is said to have met his death on the battlefield – a fact that is corroborated both by the terrible head wounds discovered on his mummy and X-ray confirmation of violent impact to the cranium.

X-ray studies have also cast doubt on some previously accepted identifications. The skeleton of the mummy thought to be that of Tuthmosis I (1504–1492 BC) has remnants of cartilage at the end of the long bones, a sign that the body was still growing at the time of death. The dead person could have been no more than eighteen – an age incompatible with the length of reign of this pharaoh. Also strange is the way the mummy's hands are placed in front of the genitalia although none of Tuthmosis' successors have their hands in this position.

In 1926 two French journalists X-rayed a mummy with a small portable X-ray machine at the Musée Guimet d'Histoire Naturelle, Lyons. The X-rays showed up an abnormal 'compact mass' in the region of the trunk; this was almost certainly a mixture of earth, resin and spices inserted in place of the viscera.

Today numerous other techniques are used in the study of mummies

Besides radiology, methods now available for studying mummies include histology (the science of organic tissues), the study of blood and tissue groups, endoscopy and a whole range of chemical and physical microanalyses. In addition there are more recent techniques such as medical imaging, in particular CT (computed tomography) scanning. Magnetic resonance imaging (MRI), on the other hand, cannot be used on mummies, since it depends on hydrogen atoms, which in the human body are found in the form of water.

Although it can provide interesting information, radiocarbon dating is not yet sufficiently precise for the purposes of estimating the exact age of human tissue. Another method, involving amino acids, can also make a contribution to this subject. It has the advantage over radiocarbon dating that it can be applied to very small samples of material, but its reliability depends on the temperature at which the material for analysis was conserved.

In the field of multidisciplinary research, several teams worldwide have conducted particularly

In 1976, 3200 years after his death, Ramesses II was taken to Paris for treatment. It was the first time that a royal mummy had left Egyptian soil and archaeologists made full use of the opportunity by subjecting it to an exhaustive examination. The X-ray of Ramesses' skull (above) shows that his brain had been removed and the cranial cavity filled with resin. His teeth were in very poor condition, which was hardly surprising: at the time of his death, Ramesses was over eighty years old.

Left

Right

Ramesses II was suffering from arteriosclerosis. The X-ray photograph (left), produced by xerography – a process, similar to photocopying, which highlights contrasting details – shows arterial calcification (visible as more or less continuous white lines) between the first and second metatarsal bones of the pharaoh's feet. This was also found in other parts of the body, notably on the carotid arteries. The photograph also showed up a fracture to the cervical spine. Although statues and images in the temples show Ramesses holding his head up very straight, even a little stiffly, the neck of his mummy (see below opposite) has a very pronounced curvature, probably caused by the embalmers. They, however, were not responsible for the fact that Ramesses' arms do not lie neatly across his chest. After thousands of years underground, when exposed to the air and the heat, the tissues of the arms have become deformed and the arms have moved out of alignment. After he had been restored and partly rebandaged Ramesses II was sterilized by radiation and replaced in the wooden coffin in which he was first found (overleaf).

worthwhile work over recent years. For instance, in the United States a team at the University of Pennsylvania led by A. Cockburn has carried out an exhaustive study of four anonymous mummies, christened PUM (Pennsylvania University Museum) I–IV. Findings for the first three mummies were rather disappointing, but PUM IV has provided a wealth of information, particularly regarding human tissue. In 1976 a French team under the direction of L. Balout and C. Roubet took on the job of restoring and studying the mummy of Ramesses II (1290–1224 BC), and an English team at the University of Manchester, led by R. David, has studied a series of seventeen mummies dating from the New Kingdom to the Graeco-Roman Period.

Anthropologists, meanwhile, have been conducting their own studies of the many skeletons discovered in the necropolises, and their findings have shown up the weakness inherent in studying mummies in museums. Both the provenance and the date of these mummies tend to be uncertain, and because of their small number and their diversity they are not representative of a natural population, unlike the large homogeneous groups studied by the anthropologists. For this reason some archaeologists have now adopted the approach of X-raying mummies on site, where they can be said to form part of a statistically uniform population.

What can be learnt from studying mummies

As regards the actual technique of mummification, all the recent studies confirm what Herodotus – almost the only, and certainly the best, written source until modern times – had to say on the subject. Mummies examined by modern archaeologists vary in terms of workmanship and quality, in line with the three categories of Herodotus. They range from those that benefited from 'first-class' techniques, which have

Roger Lichtenberg X-raying a mummy on site (at Duch) – a task that often calls for imagination and a talent for improvisation. Below: one of the Duch team's helpers cleaning sand from a mummy. This is a painstaking job that can take half a day.

This small package (left) was found between the thighs of a castrated mummy in a tomb at Duch. X-rays showed it to be the mummy of a frog – the symbol of rebirth – and not the mummy's sexual organs, as was at first supposed.

preserved the body intact and retained facial expressiveness, to those mummies, the product of more hurried or even slapdash techniques, that have deteriorated to a greater or lesser degree and are now incomplete or damaged.

Other observations tally with ritual prescriptions or what we know of myths. Some mummies are buried, for example, with their arms crossed over their chest in imitation of Osiris, god of the dead; others are castrated in allusion to the Osirian myth. Traces of gold have been found on the face and limbs of some mummies and this type of body gilding was also a (late) deification practice which was supposed to turn the dead person into an Osiris: as a ritual formula runs, 'You are regenerated by gold'.

In some cases the embalmer appears to have been simply concentrating on achieving the most attractive results. For example, he might patch together a damaged hand and where a tooth was missing insert in its place an

Gold leaf or electrum (an alloy of gold and silver) was applied to the face (above, the 'priest of Duch') or other parts of the body in the Graeco-Roman period. As a stable metal gold would have helped to prevent deterioration.

ivory one on a wooden peg. Or again he might place a small onion over an eye socket to give the dead person the appearance of sight (though this may in fact have been in accordance with ritual practices specified in the embalmers' hand-books).

The position of the disembowelling incision appears to have had no religious significance: it was originally made on the lower left-hand side of the body, at right angles to the ribs, then, following Tuthmosis III's reign (1479–1425 BC), it was cut parallel to the pubic bone. The opening was not generally sewn up. In some cases no incision was made at all and the abdominal organs were removed via the rectum.

For many years archaeologists were in doubt as to whether the natron used to desiccate the body was

The scenes depicted on sarcophagi and tombs tell us a great deal about the precise techniques used by the embalmers, though one aspect that is virtually never illustrated is the desiccation process. Below: detail from the Hildesheim sarcophagus showing a mummified body being sprinkled with water to remove any remaining natron crystals and impurities.

applied as a solution, as implied by the term 'natron bath', or in the form of crystals. It became apparent, however, from studies carried out by scholars including A. Lucas, who experimented with the mummification of pigeons, and by Dr Z. Iskander, using ducks, that it must have been natron crystals that were used (no doubt in such a way as to completely cover the body).

The ancient texts do not specify precisely what balms and unguents were used and their chemical make-up is very difficult to establish because of the profound modifications which the molecules have undergone over the course of time. They are variously referred to as 'resin', 'bitumen' (the word 'mummy' derives from an Arabic word for bitumen) and 'cedarwood oil'. The aromatic plants discovered both in and on the mummies have been easier to identify and include, among others, laurel, pepper, cistus and juniper.

I mages produced by a scanner are more precise than X-rays, particularly where soft tissue is concerned. Scanning techniques are useful for studying the thorax and the abdomen, since under X-ray the replaced viscera or the products used for stuffing the body only show up as a dark, undifferentiated mass. Above: a section of the skull of a mummy showing the block of resin inserted in place of the brain.

The existence of mummies provides a unique research opportunity for supplementing anthropological studies

Most anthropological studies relating to the ancient Egyptians have been carried out on skeletal remains, but mummies can provide a wealth of information not otherwise available. By studying hair, nails, skin and fingerprints we can learn a great deal about ethnic categories and gain a fairly good idea of what the ancient Egyptians actually looked like.

Through careful mummification even the most delicate anatomical structures are preserved. Left: enlargement of a fingertip (magnification: 3.5x) showing the fingerprint and the openings of the sweat glands.

An X-ray (opposite, top) of part of the femurs and the knee joints of a mummy, showing the lines relating to arrested growth due to malnourishment or illness. Right: the deformed left foot of the pharaoh Siptah (end of the 19th Dynasty). Experts are divided: some think it was a club foot, others a consequence of polio.

Archaeologists have now established a method of scientifically measuring the bones of mummies on site using X-rays. They have also successfully carried out studies on mummified tissue. Their findings confirm the historical hypothesis that the ancient Egyptians were descended in roughly equal measures from Berber and Semitic peoples, with an increasing Negroid influence from the north to the south of the country. What is particularly striking about the Egyptian people is that, despite various external influences at different periods of their history, they have remained remarkably unchanged to modern times.

Mummies are a much more fruitful source of information than skeletons for studying the state of health of a population

The study of X-ray photographs has also yielded useful statistics concerning the striae, or linear marks, found on bones which are evidence of arrested growth. These marks, corresponding to periods of illness or malnourishment, are frequently found on mummies analysed at the necropolis at Duch, which was in a particularly poor area, in contrast to those studied by Gray, which probably belonged to better-off sections of the population.

Other studies have established that the average life-span of people in Egypt in the first centuries AD was approximately forty – which is only a few years less than in Europe a hundred and fifty years ago. However, this figure fails to take into account the rate of deaths at birth and also the high infant mortality rate.

Dental studies show widespread abrasion of the crowns – which is hardly surprising when it is known that the ancient Egyptians ate a type of bread made with coarse flour containing silica (sand). This wearing down of the teeth led to damage to the gums and extensive abscesses. Tooth decay, on the other hand, only really became a problem fairly late on in Egyptian history, when sugar began to feature in the diet (initially only of the ruling classes). Honey had long been known and used in Egypt and was even one of the ingredients of a recommended remedy for tooth decay.

The ancient medical papyri list a number of illnesses to which the Egyptians were prone, but many of them are difficult now to identify from the texts alone. The study of mummies helps to clarify the nature of some of these illnesses and confirms the identification of others, while also pointing to the presence of some which were not mentioned in the texts. Injuries, such as fractures, are particularly easy to spot, whatever the method of examination. The same is also true for degenerative conditions like osteoarthritis, which seems to have been very widespread and to have affected mainly the spinal column. This complaint was often associated with scoliosis (the lateral curvature of the spine) and seems to have been linked with agricultural work in the fields and also carrying heavy weights.

The detection of parasitic diseases, such as bilharzia and filariasis, on the other hand, depends on X-ray examination, since scientific examinations of the tissues are liable to cause irreversible damage to the mummy. Tuberculosis and diseases of the heart and blood vessels have been identified, but cancer far less so. This must be due to the fact that cancer frequently attacks the soft organs, which are no longer available for study.

The upper jaw of a mummy from Duch, showing damage caused by abscesses.

Statuette of the protective deity Ptah Patek. Note how the dome of the skull and the trunk are fully formed, while the base of the skull and limbs are underdeveloped. This type of dwarfism was fairly common in ancient Egypt. Opposite, below: mummified head of a seven-year-old girl. The presence of the wig in which she was buried pointed to typhoid as the cause of death. Beneath the wig the child's hair had fallen out and was growing back in an irregular fashion – both features of prolonged forms of the illness.

Diagnosis: almost everyone was in poor health

The village of Duch, in the Great Oasis, was occupied between the 1st century BC and the 5th century AD. A study of nearly two hundred mummies and skeletons from the necropolis of the village has concluded that almost everyone was suffering from some medical complaint. Spinal osteoarthritis, dislocations and malnourishment (as indicated by the bone markings relating to arrested growth) were found to be the most common problems.

Occasionally clinical observations and X-ray examination were able to pinpoint the actual cause of death, as in the case of a seven-year-old girl apparently suffering from typhoid, or that of another child who died as a result of a fractured skull. Physical deprivation and hard labour, combined with an almost total lack of medical provision, were the chief causes of the villagers' almost universal poor health.

Photograph and X-ray of the damaged skull of a mummy from Duch with the mummified remains (right) of the brain, found in the skull cavity. The head had become detached from the body (a fairly common occurrence) and in order to hold it in place the embalmer had inserted a palm branch down the spine. While reattaching the head he appears to have speared it with the branch and shattered the back of the skull.

Mummies have lost none of their mystique through scientific investigation

Mummies have always been an object of fascination mixed with fear. Partly, no doubt, because they bring us face to face with death, and what we might regard as a kind of life after death (however artificial). Partly, too,

because of the exciting way in which they telescope time, bringing us into contact with individuals who lived many thousands of years ago – particularly when the individuals in question are kings who played such an important role in history as Tuthmosis III and Ramesses II. As the equivalent of ghosts and other potentially maleficent beings, mummies have found their way into the collective unconscious and have attracted to themselves their own film and literary culture. The modern image of the mummy as a baleful creature come to wreak havoc among the living in fulfilment of some ancient curse curiously echoes an obsession of the ancient Egyptians themselves, who believed that the dead could return and take revenge on the living if they held a grudge against them.

The underground cemetery of the Monastery of the Capuchins at Palermo clearly had a profound impact on the 19th-century French novelist Gustave Flaubert, who writes: 'Just imagine twelve or fifteen hundred corpses reduced to a mummified state, grimacing for all they are worth, some apparently laughing, others crying, some opening mouths like great caverns and extending a blackened tongue between two toothless jaws, others pinching their lips together convulsively, stretched, wizened, twisted, dislocated ...' The cemetery (now a museum) houses thousands of desiccated bodies, dressed in what was once their greatest finery and grouped by corridors (men, women, officials, monks). A bishop (left) presided over the priests' corridor.

Mummification is not the exclusive preserve of the religion of ancient Egypt. In the history of both East and West there is a long-standing tradition of embalming (or desiccation) – a treatment that has been extended at various times to French kings, the monks from the monasteries of Saint Catharine in the Sinai peninsula and the Capuchins in Palermo, Sicily, and many others.

Modern medicine has perfected techniques for stabilizing the body after death, allowing burial to be postponed, and in the United States a technique has been developed using liquid nitrogen as a medium for freezing the body and preserving it in anticipation of 'resurrection', when whatever was the cause of death can be cured. The ancient Egyptians might well have regarded such a restoration of life as the ultimate in mummification.

Embalming was practised by many civilizations, but only the ancient Egyptians truly mastered the art. The Andean mummy (opposite), the bishop from a monastery in Palermo (opposite, left) and the mummies from Guanajuato in Mexico (below) were produced by more or less natural desiccation. Such mummies often look like little more than clothed skeletons. Overleaf: mourners in the tomb of Ramose.

DOCUMENTS

Funeral rites

The majority of funerary texts have been found in the tombs themselves. They are mainly religious texts, but in among them is the odd civil document, such as a funeral account.

M ask and cartonnage of a Middle Kingdom mummy (11th Dynasty).

The *Book of the Dead*: the declaration of innocence

During the New Kingdom it became customary to place in the tomb, somewhere near the body, a scroll of papyrus containing texts whose purpose was to prepare the dead person for the afterlife. The Book of the Dead, *as these rather stereotyped texts were known, can be traced back directly to the Middle Kingdom Coffin Texts, themselves derived from the Pyramid Texts. The texts are intended as both a guide for the dead person in the journey in the afterlife and a collection of magic formulas designed to ensure safe passage through that other world. Chapter 125, which relates to the psychostasia or 'Weighing of the Heart' ceremony, is particularly famous. During this ceremony the dead assert their innocence in the presence of Osiris, and if they succeed in passing the test they are said to be 'justified'.*

Homage to thee, O Great God, thou Lord of double Maati, I have come to thee, O my Lord, and I have brought myself hither that I may behold thy beauties. I know thee, and I know thy name, and I know the name[s] of the two and forty gods who exist with thee in this Hall of double Maati, who live as warders of sinners and who feed on their blood on the day when the lives of men are taken into account in the presence of the god Un-nefer. ...
I have not done evil to mankind. I have not oppressed the members of my family, I have not wrought evil in the place of right and truth. I have not had knowledge of worthless men. I have wrought no evil. I have not thought scorn of god. I have not defrauded the oppressed one of his property. I have

not done that which is an abomination unto the gods. I have not caused harm to be done to the servant by his chief. I have not caused pain, I have made no man to suffer hunger. I have made no one to weep. I have done no murder. I have not given the order for murder to be done for me. I have not inflicted pain upon mankind. I have not defrauded the temples of their oblations. I have not purloined the cakes of the gods. I have not carried off the cakes offered to the *khus*. I have not committed fornication. I have not polluted myself … nor diminished from the bushel. I have neither added to nor filched away land. I have not encroached upon the fields. I have not added to the weights of the scales. I have not mis-read the pointer of the scales. I have not carried away the milk from the mouths of children. I have not driven away the cattle which were upon their pastures … I am pure, I am pure, I am pure, I am pure!… therefore let not evil befall me in this land and in this Hall of the double Maati, because I, even I, know the name[s] of these gods who are therein …

The deceased then addresses each of the forty-two assessor deities

Hail, thou crusher of bones who
  cometh forth from Suten-henen,
  I have not uttered falsehood …
Hail, thou who goest backwards, who
  comes forth from the city of Bast,
  I have never pried into matters …
Hail, thou lord of two horns, who
  cometh forth from Satiu, I have not
  multiplied my speech overmuch.…
                    The Book of the Dead
                    E.A.Wallis Budge, 1898

Extract from an embalming ritual

The technical and religious aspects of embalming were governed by strict rules that were set out in the ritual texts. One of these texts has come down to us in the form of two copies from the Graeco-Roman Period found in the necropolis at Thebes. The original was undoubtedly much older. Though incomplete, the text covers the various stages of the bandaging process together with the invocatory formulas designed to accompany the different stages. The gulf between the real and the ideal – as embodied in this protocol – becomes only too apparent when one comes to study the mummies themselves.

VI
Fitting the fingerstalls to the hands and feet
Following on from this, fit the golden fingerstalls to his hands and feet. Begin with the ends of the four fingers and finish with the left thumb [?]. Wrap with a long piece of red linen from Sais.

Words to be spoken following these procedures:
    Osiris N [name of the dead person]! You have just received your gold fingerstalls and your fingers are pure gold and your nails are electrum! You are touched, in truth, by the emanation of Re, the divine body of Osiris! Your legs will carry you to the eternal abode and your hands will carry for you as far as the place of infinite duration, for you are regenerated by gold and revived by electrum. Your fingers will glitter in the abode of Osiris, in the embalming workshop of Horus himself…

VII

Second unction and wrapping of the head
… Anoint both his head and his
mouth, each with oil for 'reattaching
the head and reattaching the face'. Bind
with the cloth of Re'-Harakhty of
Heliopolis. The cloth of Nekhbet of el-
Kab should be placed on top of his
head; the cloth of Hathor, lady of
Dendera, on his face and that of Thoth,
who separates the Two Combatants, on
his ears; the cloth of Nebet-Hetepet on
the nape of his neck.…

Twenty-two rolls for the right and
the left of the face, to be wound at the
level of his ears.…

Then, following this, bind very
carefully with a bandage of two fingers'
width.…

Words to be spoken following this:
Venerable and Great One, lady of the
West, sovereign of the East, come,
penetrate to the ears of Osiris N!…

Make him see with his eye and hear
with his ears; make him breathe with
his nose and speak with his mouth;
make him use his tongue to argue
inside the Douat!

Rituels funéraires de l'Ancienne Egypte
J.-C. Goyon, 1972

Harpist's Song

*The funerary texts inscribed in New
Kingdom tombs often included what has
been called the 'Harpist's Song'. With
slight variations, the song always treats
the same themes, in particular the
transitoriness of human life. While not
denying the reality of the 'second life', it
stresses the impossibility of going back and
the importance of 'living a happy day' – of
making the most of this life while waiting
to enter the 'land that loves silence'. In
other words, the harpist's song is the
Egyptian version of a common theme:
'seize the day'.*

For a generation passes,
and another remains, since the time of
the ancestors,
those gods who existed aforetime,
who rest in their pyramids,
and the blessed noble dead likewise,
buried in their pyramids.
The builder of chapels, their places are
no more.
What has become of them?
I have heard the words of Imhotep and
Hordedef,
whose sayings are so told:
What of their places? Their walls have
fallen;
their places are no more, like those who
never were.
None returns from there to tell their
conditions,
to tell their state, to reassure us,
until we attain the place where they
have gone.
May you be happy with this,

Harpist performing a lament for a dead
person.

forgetfulness giving you benediction.
Follow your heart while you live!
Put myrrh on your head!
Clothe yourself with fine linen!
Anoint yourself with true wonders of
the divine rite!
Increase your happiness!
Be not weary-hearted! Follow your
heart and happiness!
Make your things on earth! Do not
destroy your heart,
until that day of lamentation comes for
you!
The weary-hearted does not hear their
lamentation; mourning cannot save a
man from the tomb-pit.
Make holiday! Do not weary of it!
Look, no one can take his things with
him.
Look, no one who has gone there
returns again.

> *Voices from Ancient Egypt. An Anthology
> of Middle Kingdom Writings*
> R.B. Parkinson, 1991

A breakdown of funeral expenses

*Papyri from the Graeco-Roman Period
contain several accounts detailing funeral
expenses. The following text was found in
a village in the Fayuum called
Soknopaiou Nesos. The major costs in this
case relate to the fabric for dressing the
mummy and the funerary mask.*

P ot for embalming oil.

	[drachmas]	[obols]
.....	12 dr	2 ob
Earthenware pot		2 ob
Red paint	4 dr	19 ob
Wax	12 dr	
Myrrh	4 dr	4 ob
Song [dirge?]		4 ob
Tallow		8 ob
Linen clothes	36 dr	16 ob

Mask	64 dr	
Cedar oil	41 dr	
Medicament for linen	4 dr	
Good oil	4 dr	
Turbon's wages	8 dr	
Lamp wicks	24 dr	
Cost of an old tunic		24 ob
Sweet wine		20 ob
Barley	16 dr	
Leaven	4 dr	
Dog	8 dr	
Little mask [?]	14 dr	
2 artabae of loaves	21 dr	
Pine cone		8 ob
Weepers	32 dr	
Carriage by donkey	8 dr	
Chaff [?]		12 ob
TOTAL	**440 dr**	**16 ob**

[The total is in fact wrong.]

> Quoted in: G. Elliot Smith
> and Warren R. Dawson,
> *Egyptian Mummies*, 1924

Mummification as described by Herodotus

Towards the middle of the 5th century BC the Greek historian Herodotus visited Egypt (then a province of the Persian empire), eager to learn all he could about the country.

Though disparaged in certain quarters ('Herodotus is a liar', according to one critic), his account of his travels includes some remarkable observations. Much of what he describes he witnessed with his own eyes; other information he gathered where possible from 'the experts'. His description of the mummification process is our principal source of information and has been largely corroborated by modern research.

In this occupation certain persons employ themselves regularly and inherit this as a craft....Then they after they have agreed for a certain price depart out of the way, and the others being left behind in the building embalm according to the best of these ways thus: first with a crooked iron tool they draw out the brain through the nostrils, extracting it partly thus and partly by pouring in drugs; and after this with a sharp stone of Ethiopia they make a cut along the side and take out the whole contents of the belly, and when they have cleared out the cavity and cleansed it with palm wine they cleanse it again with spices pounded up: then they fill the belly with pure myrrh pounded up and with cassia and other spices except frankincense, and sew it together again. Having so done they keep it for embalming covered up in natron for seventy days but for a longer time than this is not permitted to embalm it; and when the seventy days are past, they wash the corpse and roll its whole body up in fine linen cut into bands, smearing these beneath with gum, which the Egyptians use generally instead of glue. Then the kinsfolk receive it from them and have a wooden figure made in the shape of a man, and when they have had this made they

Bust of Herodotus (opposite). Above: sarcophagus said to have belonged to 'Alexander', lithograph, in W. Alexander, *Egyptian Monuments*, 1805.

enclose the corpse, and having shut it up within, they store it in a sepulchral chamber, setting it to stand upright against the wall. Thus they deal with the corpses which are prepared in the most costly way; but for those who desire the middle way and wish to avoid great cost they prepare the corpse as follows: having filled their syringes with the oil which is got from cedar-wood, with this they forthwith fill the belly of the corpse, and this they do without having either cut it open or taken out the bowels, but they inject the oil by the breech, and, having stopped the drench from returning back they keep it then the appointed number of days for embalming, and on the last of these days they let the cedar oil come out from the belly, which they before put in, and it has such power that it brings out with it the bowels and interior organs of the body dissolved; and the natron dissolves the flesh, so that there is left of the corpse only the skin and the bones. When they have done this they give back the corpse at once in that condition without working upon it any more. The third kind of embalming, by which are prepared the bodies of those who have less means is as follows: they cleanse out the body with a purge and then keep the body for embalming during the seventy days, and at once after that they give it back to the bringers to carry away.

The History of Herodotus, Book II
Translated by G.C. Macaulay, 1890

Poor mummies!

There have always been looters, and collectors, eager to lay their hands on whatever riches a tomb might house, and no mummies – illustrious or anonymous – have enjoyed the peace to which they were supposedly entitled.

The creation of the new solar disc, painting in Ramesses VI's burial chamber.

The pillaging of the royal tombs under Ramesses IX

Under Ramesses I and II (19th Dynasty) Egypt regained the glory it had lost when its capital shifted to el-'Amarna, but after Ramesses III the 20th Dynasty witnessed a gradual decline in royal power and a corresponding increase in the power of the priesthood. Emboldened by the political unrest, during Ramesses IX's reign looters extended their activities to include the royal tombs near Thebes. The mayor of Thebes, whose name was Paser, opened an enquiry, which was to lead to the arrest and trial of several robbers. The following is an extract from the report drawn up by the commission of enquiry.

The pyramid-tomb of King Sekhemre Shedtaui, son of Re Sobekemsaf. It was found to have been violated by the thieves by tunnelling in the nfrw-chamber of its pyramid from the outer hall of the rock tomb of Nebamun, overseer of the granary of King Menkheperre. The burial-chamber of the king was found empty of its lord and likewise the burial-chamber of the great royal wife, Nubkhaas his consort, the thieves having laid their hands on them. The vizier, the notables and the butlers investigated the matter, and the nature of the attack which the thieves had made on this king and his consort was discovered....

T.E. Peet
The Great Tomb-Robberies of the Twentieth Egyptian Dynasty, 1930

Extract from the robbers' statement:

We went to rob tombs in accordance with our regular habit, we found the pyramid of King Sekhemre-shedtawy, son of Re Sebekemsaf, this being not at all like the pyramids and tombs of the nobles which we habitually went to rob. We took our copper tools and we broke into this pyramid of this king through its innermost part. We found its underground chambers and we took lighted candles in our hands and we went down. Then we broke through the rubble that we found at the mouth of his recess and found this god lying at the back of his burial-place. And we found the burial-place of Queen Nubkhaas, his queen, situated beside him, it being protected and guarded by plaster and covered with rubble. This we also broke through and found her [resting] there in similar fashion. We opened their sarcophagi and their coffins in which they were, and found the noble mummy of this king equipped with a falchion; a large number of amulets and jewels of gold were upon his neck, and his head-piece of gold was upon him. The noble mummy of this king was completely bedecked with gold, and his coffins were adorned with gold and silver inside and out and inlaid with all sorts of precious stones. We collected the gold we found on the noble mummy of this god, together with his amulets and jewels which were on his neck and [that on] the coffins in which he was resting, [and we] found the queen in exactly the same state. We collected all that we found upon her likewise and set fire to their coffins. We took their furniture which we found with them consisting of articles of gold, silver and bronze, and divided them among ourselves. And we made into eight parts the gold which we found on these two gods coming from their mummies, amulets, jewels and coffins and 20 *deben* of gold

fell to each of the eight of us, making 160 *deben* of gold, the fragments of furniture not being included. Then we crossed over to Thebes.

A.J. Spencer
Death in Ancient Egypt, 1982

The acquisition and sale of Egyptian antiquities by a European in the 19th century

In the 19th century both England and France were engaged in the collection of Egyptian antiquities, which often led to rivalry over the best pieces. For England, the Consul-General, Henry Salt (1780–1827), was aided by Giovanni Belzoni (1778–1823), the 'Patagonian Samson' (although he was born in Padua). With Belzoni's help Henry Salt put together three large collections of pieces. The first was bought by the British Museum in London, the second was acquired by the King of France and is now in the Louvre. The third collection was sold after Salt's death by Sotheby's and again a great deal of it was bought by the British Museum. Salt's interpreter and agent was Giovanni d'Athanasi, who wrote his memoirs of his experiences in Egypt.

In the excavations at Abydos we do not find any great variety of mummies – they are chiefly of one kind, and enclosed in wooden cases. The tombs in the plain are all lined with a coating of brick-work, arched at the top and covered with plaister [sic], a precaution rendered indispensable by reason of the friable nature of the sandy rock which predominates in the neighbourhood. On the four walls of the principal chamber are compartments expressly provided for the reception of the usual tablets and statues, and on the pavement are sarcophagi of calcareous stone of ordinary workmanship. These chambers do not contain more than two or three of these sarcophagi....The tablets and idols, and other objects found with the mummies in these tombs are all of the same style. Those who ransacked the tombs in search of gold and silver, have succeeded so well in obtaining access even to the uttermost chambers, that I have not had the good fortune to find a single tomb in these parts which had not been opened before, and of course those that I did enter were knocked about and injured by those who had preceded me.

During the whole of my sojourn in Abydos I only found two mummies in an untouched and perfect state, which were contained in cases of very ordinary make. These two cases are now in London, one of them belonging, I believe, to Mr Sams, who bought it of me with some other articles of antiquity when he was in Egypt.

A circumstance which I regard as peculiarly interesting with respect to the tombs at Abydos, is that all the mummies are embalmed after the same manner, and with one kind of balm, instead of different materials as is the case at Thebes. At Abydos the bodies are universally found preserved with the black balm which I have already mentioned; at least in the course of all our excavations we did not find one of any other kind. This would lead one to believe that the black embalment was the first in point of antiquity of all that the ancients adopted. Mr Salt's opinion, which is also concurred in by Mr Wilkinson, was that the city of Abydos was more ancient than Thebes.

To his account of his adventures in Egypt, Athanasi added a catalogue of the sale of Salt's third collection, with a short introduction. A total of 1270 lots, of many different kinds of objects, made up the sale. The total amount reached by the entire collection was £7,168 18s 6d.

Three Collections of Egyptian Antiquities were formed by the late Mr Salt during his residence, as Consul-General in Egypt. On his arrival in that country in the year 1816, he found that Monsieur Drouetti, formerly the French consul, was in Upper Egypt, busily employed in buying up every thing that might add to the Collection of Antiquities which he had been several years in forming, with the view of disposing of them to the French Government.

The following is one particular lot in the sale:

150 The Mummy of a Female of high quality, 5 feet 4 in. high, with its case, highly painted and ornamented...£105.

The mask of this Mummy, which is highly ornamented, presents us with a beautiful specimen of that art and elegance oftentimes so admirably displayed by the Ancient Egyptians in their delineation of the human countenance.

The arms are folded across the body, and on the fingers of the left hand are nine cornelian and other rings, those of the right having thereon three. The whole of the upper part of the body and head was ornamented with wreaths of the sun flower, which were, according to the custom, only placed on the mummified bodies of those persons that were unmarried. These ornaments fell to pieces soon after the opening of the case.

In front of the body are attached two tablets, the first in silver and gold work, representing a jackal on a pedestal; the other, of similar work having in the centre a Scarabeus of stone…with seven lines of hieroglyphics, on either side of a priest with uplifted hands, and on the top the emblem of the soul with extended wings. In the inside of the case is the platted [sic] hair of the deceased enveloped in cloth, and also a small idol, in the form of a mummy, with silver work.

This is one of the most curious and interesting Mummies extant, and doubtless contains all the numerous rings as represented on the fingers, and other beautiful ornaments.

Giovanni d'Athanasi
A Brief Account of the Researches and Discoveries in Upper Egypt, Made under the Direction of Henry Salt, Esq.
1836

A European visiting a tomb in the company of local Arabs, engraving, c. 1860.

Two sensational discoveries

Systematic exploration of Egypt during the last century brought its rewards, leading to the discovery of a number of royal tombs. Illustrious pharaohs saw the light of day once more and mummies became an important focus of research.

A labaster vases found in Tutankhamun's tomb.

The discovery of the cache at Deir el-Bahari

In 1875 the antiquities market in Luxor began selling objects clearly originating from royal tombs. Archaeologists took note and in 1881 Gaston Maspero, newly-appointed director of the Antiquities Service, decided to open an enquiry. Suspicion soon fell on a family living in the village of Gourna, the Abd el-Rassul brothers. Under insistent questioning one of the brothers finally broke his silence and revealed the existence of a hiding place stashed full of mummies.

On Wednesday [5 July] Mohammed Ahmed Abd el-Rassul took Emil Brugsch and Ahmed Effendi Kamal to the place where the burial vault was located. The Egyptian engineer originally responsible for tunnelling the vault had designed it with the utmost skill: no hiding place was ever better concealed.

At the bottom of the shaft, a corridor 1.40 m wide by 0.80 m high was tunnelled in the west wall. After 7.40 m the corridor turns sharply to the north and continues in that direction for approximately 60 m, though its dimensions vary: at certain points it is as much as 2 m wide, at others only 1.30 m. About halfway along, five or six roughly hewn steps mark a drop in the level of the floor and on the right-hand side an unfinished niche of sorts shows that another change in direction had originally been planned. The gallery finally opens into a kind of irregular oblong chamber, about 80 m long.

The first thing Emil Brugsch saw when he arrived at the bottom of the shaft was a white and yellow coffin bearing the name Nibsonu. The coffin was in the corridor, about 0.60 m from the entrance. A little further on was a coffin whose shape recalled the style of the 17th Dynasty; next to it lay the coffin of Queen Tiuhathor Honttoui; next to that Seti I's. Scattered all over the floor alongside the coffins were boxes of funerary statuettes, Canopic jars and bronze libation vases and, right at the back, in the angle made by the corridor as it turns north, Queen Isimkheb's funeral tent, folded and crumpled as if it were an object of no value – no doubt carelessly thrown in the corner by a priest in a hurry to leave. The main corridor was equally cluttered and chaotic and we had to crawl along it without knowing where we were putting our hands and feet. The coffins and the mummies, glimpsed in the candlelight, bore historic names: among them, Amenophis I and Tuthmos [Tuthmosis] II (in the niche by the stairs), Ahmose [Amosis] I and his son Siamun, Soqnunri [Seqenenre], Queen Ahhotpu [Aahotep] and Ahmose Nofritari [Ahmose Nefertari]. The end chamber was the most jumbled of all, but here the style was predominantly that of the 20th Dynasty, recognizable at a glance. Mohammed Ahmed Abd el-Rassul's story, which had seemed fanciful at first, scarcely did justice to the truth: where I had expected to meet one or two petty kings, the Arabs had uncovered a whole vault full of kings. And what kings! Perhaps the most famous in the history of Egypt – Thutmos [Tuthmosis] III and Seti I, Ahmose [Amosis] the Liberator and Ramesses II the Conqueror. Emil Brugsch thought he must be dreaming, stumbling unexpectedly into such company, and when I see, and touch, the bodies of so many illustrious

The mummy of Seti I, discovered in the royal cache at Deir el-Bahari.

persons we never imagined could be more than names to us, like him I still find it hard to believe that I am not dreaming.

Two hours sufficed for this initial examination, then the removal work began. The mudir's men swiftly assembled three hundred Arabs and these men set to work.... Mohammed went down the shaft and organized the removal procedure from there, while Emil Brugsch and Ahmed Effendi Kamal took charge of the objects as they came to the surface, transported them to the foot of the hill and lay them alongside one another, keeping a close eye on everything as they did so. Emptying the tomb took 48 hours of hard labour, but the job was only half done then. We still had to take the goods across the Theban plain and over the river to Luxor. Some of the coffins required twelve to sixteen men to lift them, and even then it was a tremendous struggle, and it took the men seven or eight hours to get from the mountain to the river. It is not hard to imagine what such a journey was like in the dust and the July heat. Finally, on the evening of the 11th, the mummies and the coffins were all in Luxor, duly wrapped in cloth and matting. Three days later the museum's steamer arrived and as soon as it was loaded left again for Bulaq with its cargo of kings. Then a strange thing happened. From Luxor to Kuft, on either bank of the Nile, dishevelled peasant women followed the boat howling like animals and the men fired shots in the way that they do at a funeral.

Gaston Maspero
La Trouvaille de Deir el-Bahari
1881

The opening of Tutankhamun's sarcophagus

On 4 November 1922, after several years spent scouring the Valley of the Kings, Howard Carter discovered the tomb of Tutankhamun, but the long and painstaking process of opening the sarcophagus and the three coffins that lay inside it only began on 10 October 1925.

This great gilded wooden coffin, 7 feet 4 in. in length, anthropoid in shape, wearing the Khat head-dress, with face and hands in heavier sheet-gold, is of Rishi type [named for the decoration imitating feathered wings]....

It was a moment as anxious as exciting. The lid came up fairly readily, revealing a second magnificent anthropoid coffin, covered with a thin gossamer linen sheet, darkened and much decayed. Upon this linen shroud were lying floral garlands, composed of olive and willow leaves, petals of the blue lotus and cornflowers, whilst a small wreath of similar kind had been placed, also over the shroud, on the emblems of the forehead. Underneath this covering, in places, glimpses could be obtained of rich multi-coloured glass decoration encrusted upon the fine gold-work of the coffin....

Further records having been taken, I was then able to remove the chaplet and garlands, and roll back the covering shroud. It was one more exciting moment. We could now gaze, with admiring eyes, upon the finest example of the ancient coffin-maker's art ever yet seen – Osiride, again in form, but most delicate in conception, and very beautiful in line....

This revealed a third coffin which, like its predecessors, was Osiride in form, but the main details and the workmanship were hidden by a close-fitting reddish-coloured linen shroud. The burnished gold face was bare; placed over the neck and breast was an elaborate bead and floral collarette, sewn upon a backing of papyrus, and tucked immediately above the Nemes head-dress was a linen napkin.

Mr Burton at once made his photographic records. I then removed the floral collarette and linen coverings. An astounding fact was disclosed. This third coffin, 6 feet 1 3/4 of an inch in length, was made of solid gold!...

But the ultimate details of the ornamentation were hidden by a black lustrous coating due to liquid unguents that had evidently been profusely poured over the coffin....The lid was raised by its golden handles and the mummy of the king disclosed....

Before us, occupying the whole of the interior of the golden coffin, was an impressive, neat and carefully made mummy, over which had been poured anointing unguents as in the case of the outside of its coffin – again in great quantity – consolidated and blackened by age. In contradistinction to the general dark and sombre effect, due to these unguents, was a brilliant, one might say magnificent, burnished gold mask or similitude of the king, covering his head and shoulders, which, like the feet, had been intentionally avoided when using the unguents. The mummy was fashioned to symbolize Osiris. The beaten gold mask, a beautiful and unique specimen of ancient portraiture, bears a sad but calm expression suggestive of youth overtaken prematurely by death.... The burnished gold hands, crossed over the breast, separate from the mask, were sewn to the material of the linen wrappings, and grasped the Flagellum and Crozier – the emblems of Osiris....

Though the attributes upon this mummy are those of the gods, the likeness is certainly that of Tut.ankh.Amen, comely and placid, with the features recognizable on all his statues and coffins....

When the detailed photographic records were made by Mr Burton, we were better able to make a closer examination of the actual state of things, and the preservation of the mummy. The greater part of the flagellum and crozier was completely decomposed, and had already fallen to dust; the threads that once held the hands and trappings in place upon the outer linen covering, were decayed, and in consequence the various sections fell apart at the slightest touch.... The farther we proceeded the more evident it became that the covering wrapping and the mummy were in a parlous state. They were completely carbonized by the action that had been set up by the fatty acids of the unguents with which they had been saturated.

Howard Carter
The Tomb of Tut.ankh.Amen, 1927

Howard Carter removing the funeral couch from Tutankhamun's tomb.

Mummies under X-ray

Röntgen's discovery of X-rays in 1895 provided a way of studying mummies without damaging them. The only problem was a logistical one: how to bring mummy, radiologist and equipment together in one place.

What does the X-ray of a mummy show?

In 1926 two journalists from the popular scientific magazine Je sais tout *expressed their surprise that the mummy of Tutankhamun, whose tomb had been discovered four years earlier, had not been X-rayed. (It was in fact, but much later.) Unconvinced by the alleged difficulties of X-raying a mummy, the two journalists decided to experiment. The Louvre was unable to supply them with a mummy, so they approached the Musée Guimet in Lyons, where Professor Moret directed them towards the mummy of a female musician.*

As for our X-ray machine, we should point out straight away that the X-ray was done with one of those modern machines designed literally for travelling with, since M. Bonin, at the Musée Guimet, lifted it (weighing scarcely 50 g) out of a sort of suitcase. Alas, there is no electricity supply in this beautiful museum…. No matter. M. Bonin's case also contained 50 metres of lead, which we simply connected up to a light socket on the floor below….

There was one preliminary test which we had to do, upon which the success or failure of our entire experiment could be said to depend: a fluoroscopy. In other words, before we could hope to obtain a sensitive plate printed with the X-ray image, it was essential to ascertain that the rays could produce an image on a simple fluorescent screen….

Despite the thickness of the table and the web of bandages, the beam of strange rays penetrated through to the fluorescent plate, and on the lighted background of the plate we saw two long dark streaks appear, then two shorter ones: the mummy's tibias and fibias!...

The two journalists carry out the X-ray proper

It took us several hours and we had to proceed by trial and error, dealing with each problem as it occurred. The first thing to understand is that our X-ray was completed in 'sections': the light source was directed from above this time, while we slid the sensitive plates under each of the different parts of the body in turn – head, neck, trunk, pelvis, etc. But what a lot of little problems kept cropping up!...

The X-rays were interpreted by the joint efforts of a surgeon, Professor G. Lardennois, and an Egyptologist, Professor Moret – evidence of the dual interest, anthropological and Egyptological, of this type of research....

'I don't know how to congratulate you enough on your bizarre initiative,' this eminent surgeon said to us. 'There is certainly a great deal to be learnt from studies of this kind. Your X-ray provides all sorts of useful anthropological information. The forehead is wide and the head well formed, showing that your Egyptian was undoubtedly an intelligent woman. Her general skeletal make-up – which has no flaws or fractures that I can identify – is that of a healthy, and I would go so far as to say "sporty", individual.

'There is one striking thing, however, and that is the abnormal distension to the thorax.... I suspect this must be because the embalmers stuffed the chest cavity, and quite energetically too....'

X-ray of a child's mummy by P.H.K. Gray. The embalmers have stuffed the abdomen with rubble to prevent the body from sagging.

M. Moret, professor at the Collège de France, had been particularly recommended to us for his knowledge of Egyptology....

Professor Moret explained that during mummification the cavities of the body – first emptied of the viscera – were indeed stuffed very vigorously....

'The X-rays produced by your machine were able to penetrate most areas of the body, but in the trunk they struck a compact mass, which shows up in black on your photograph. What is this mass – this thick stuffing – you may wonder. It is almost certainly a mixture of earth, resin and aromatic plants. It may also be that the embalmers replaced the dead woman's viscera....

'What a lot of interesting things your X-ray photograph shows!... Yes, the archaeologist gains new insights and clarification from your X-ray, and it is to be hoped that closer and closer links will be established between the different sciences – however dissimilar their objectives may appear – to the advantage of each.'

C. Leleux and M. Gouineau,
Je sais tout
No. 243, March 1926;
No. 244, April 1926

The largest series of mummies X-rayed

During the 1960s P.H.K. Gray X-rayed 133 Egyptian mummies (88 of them adults) in a number of European museums, notably in the United Kingdom and the Netherlands. His studies remain to this day the most extensive of their kind. In a brief review of all such studies carried out to date Gray expresses surprise that X-raying was still a relatively rare approach, even where detailed work was being done. G.E. Smith and F. Wood-Jones devoted a large part of their efforts to the general anatomy of mummies and M.A. Ruffer (1921) and A.T. Sandison (1963) concentrated on histological aspects. In either case the mummies were taken apart and dissected, and necessarily destroyed in the process.

And yet shortly after the discovery of X-rays the importance of their application to Egyptology had already been demonstrated by Flinders Petrie, who published excellent photographs of the lower limbs of some of his mummies. One of these X-rays shows clearly defined lines at the lower extremity of a tibia corresponding to a period of arrested growth. In 1931, moreover, R.L. Moodie had given a brief description of his X-ray studies on seventeen Egyptian mummies.

Since radiography has no deleterious effect on a wrapped mummy, and in view of the paucity of reports on the radiologic examination of mummies, it was thought worthwhile to obtain permission to radiograph the specimens in the museums of Great Britain and other European countries. The objectives were to determine the presence or absence of human bones; to determine the age and the sex of the person; to correlate the radiographic findings with the various embalming technics; to demonstrate amulets within the wrappings; and to demonstrate pathological changes....

Gray elaborates on the various aspects which the use of X-rays on mummies can illuminate

X-ray of a child's skull by Gray superimposed on the mummy's mask.

Archaeology: determination of the presence or absence of human bones. The large museums of Great Britain and other European countries contain many mummies purchased in Egypt by early nineteenth-century explorers and travellers. The native dealers were quick to realise that a good profit could be made from the sale of 'souvenirs' and mummies – forgeries were by no means uncommon In 1837, [C.R.] Scott wrote: ' for the eagerness with which every sort of trash is purchased makes the trade a very profitable concern, and opens a wide door for fraud by the encouragement it gives to the manufacture of mummies'. This study has confirmed Scott's statement. On many an occasion, a traveller had been sold not a mummy, but a modern fake.

Determination of age and sex. A coffin can usually be dated by its orthography and style, but it cannot be assumed that the coffin contains its original inhabitant. For example, a coffin bearing the names and the titles of a man may contain the mummy of a woman, and vice versa.

In one case a specimen appeared to be the unwrapped mummy of a woman 75 years old. Radiography, however, showed it to be that of a girl about 17 years old.

Correlation of radiographic findings with known embalming technics. It has been possible to correlate radiographic findings with known embalming technics, especially in mummies of the Twenty-first Dynasty, wherein the salient features are visceral packs within the body cavity, artificial eyes, and subcutaneous plumping of the body.

Demonstration of amulets. Being radiopaque, the amulets can be detected easily, and when desirable can be and have been localised with ease and removed through small incisions in the wrappings.

Palaeopathology. Moodie pointed out, 'Roentgenology supplements all other methods of learning of physical troubles in early times.' It was originally thought that only bony lesions would be found. Such, however, was not the case.

Osteoarthritis. Osteoarthritis of the vertical column was common.

Lines of arrested growth. These were present in a little over 30 percent of the 133 mummies examined.

Fractures. Numerous fractures and dislocations were found, especially in late-period mummies, but they were nearly all postmortem.

Other bony features. The state of the feet indicates that restrictive footwear was not worn.

Dental condition. Dental disease and attrition were found to be very common.

Lesions of soft tissue. Among the 27 mummies in the museum at Leiden, 20 are those of adults. In at least four of these, there was extensive calcification of the arteries of the legs.

Gallstones were almost certainly present in one of the 133 mummies and were possibly present in another....

Important diseases not found. No evidence of the following important diseases was found in the skeletons of the mummies: malignant neoplasia, tuberculosis, syphilis, leprosy or rickets.

P.H.K. Gray
'Radiography of Ancient Egyptian Mummies'
Medical Radiography and Photography,
Vol. 43, no.2, 1967

Ramesses II in Paris

The Ramesses II operation represents the high point of the studies conducted on museum-based mummies. In 1975, following an agreement between the French and Egyptian governments, the mummy of Ramesses was taken to Paris for treatment. The mummy was received with the honours due to a head of state. Thanks to the methods used the pharaoh's remains were subjected to the most thorough examinations without incurring any damage.

In 1912 X-rays taken by G.E. Smith had shown that the mummy was deteriorating and it now needed urgent attention. Numerous methods were used, including radiology. X-rays were to reveal not only a number of pathological changes, but also the presence of artifacts resulting from the embalming process. Simple X-ray examination led to the conclusion that Ramesses II had suffered a fracture to the cervical spine during the embalming process, at the precise moment, in fact, when the resin was being poured into his cranial cavity.

A typical portrait of Ramesses II (Louvre, Paris) with his head held high.

From the moment of his arrival in Paris, scientists worked assiduously to save Ramesses. The first task was to determine the exact cause of his illness. Among the remains of the linen wrappings, some samples of minute fragments from the mummy's chest and some fallen hairs were collected and immediately analysed in the specialized laboratories of the Musée d'Histoire Naturelle, the Identité Judicaire, the Institut Textile de France, L'Oreal, the CNRS and the Commissariat à l'Energie Atomique. Was it bacteria? Fungus? Insects? the experts all brought their most sophisticated microscopes to bear on the problem....It was Dr Jean Mouchacca, a cryptogram specialist at the Musée d'Histoire Naturelle, who succeeded in identifying the destructive organism: a fungus with the preposterous name of *Daedalea biennis Fries.*....

The in-depth study of Ramesses' skeleton, the walls of his femoral arteries, his teeth, and his whole mummified body, proved highly revealing. It appears that Ramesses suffered from a slight limp and a stiffening of the spinal column, and that his head was inclined too far forward in relation to his spine. When he was buried, the embalmers straightened his head, causing visible fracturing to the front and back of his neck. The pharaoh had numerous abscesses in his teeth and all the evidence suggests that he died as a result of a general infection.

Uncovering the cause of Ramesses' illness was one thing; saving him was quite another. Lionel Balout and

Colette Roubet knew this only too well. It was time to act and to arrest the problem using all the means that modern technology placed at their disposal. Chemotherapy, and any kind of treatment using heat or cold, were quickly dismissed as possibilities. The reason for this was that no one knew how the resins and gums employed during the embalming process would react to such treatments: there were too many imponderables. Only one solution remained: to subject Ramesses II to radiation treatment. It was a difficult decision for which to take sole responsibility. If the pharaoh were even the slightest bit damaged, diplomatic relations with the Egyptians would no doubt suffer.

From the start of the operation the mummy was handled with the utmost care and remained under the watchful eye of Dr Sawki Nakhla, Egypt's official representative. The base of the oak coffin, the vehicle in which the king had been travelling, was cut away so that a sheet of altuglas could be slid under the body and this then transferred to an operating table. The head and torso were propped up with small cushions to avoid putting any strain on the skeleton, and the body was only exposed while the scientists were working on it, and then never for more than three hours at a stretch....

The key word, therefore, was caution. The scientists had no option but to take action, however. Jean Mouchacca's diagnosis was quite explicit: if they failed to eradicate the fungus, by the end of the century Ramesses II's mummy would be entirely eaten up by it. Balout alone was in a position to decide on the form of treatment that should be applied: radiation....

Ramesses II was first restored, with infinite care, by the specialists at the Musée de l'Homme, then draped in a piece of antique linen cloth courtesy of the Louvre and placed in his cedarwood coffin. He had been reborn a second time and recovered all his former radiance. The doctors who tended him merely played the same part that the priests had played before them. Respecting ancient tradition, they had given Ramesses's spirit the dwelling it desired: a perfect body. And from within this frail frame the king now gazes down on the river of life.

Sygma

Drawings by R. Lichtenberg showing the position of Ramesses' head before the cervical fracture (top right) and after it (left and bottom right).

The ruins of Duch (above) and (right) some of the 700 mummies exhumed there (see also pages 1–9).

The mummies from the necropolis at Duch: evidence collected from recent investigations

The mummies in the museums are often of unknown provenance and have essentially been selected for their careful workmanship and good condition. Studying mummies on site is a better way of sampling a population as a whole.

In 1976 Serge Sauneron, director of the Institut Français d'Archéologie Orientale in Cairo, obtained a concession to carry out excavations at Duch, a village in the extreme south of the Kharga Oasis, in the Libyan desert. The site had been known since the beginning of the 19th century, but never investigated. And yet it had much to commend it: a stone temple, almost intact, surrounded by a huge unfired brick enclosure, a temple built of unfired brick, the remains of a village whose inhabitants must have numbered around 5000 at the height of its prosperity, and a vast necropolis. The site is known to have been occupied between the 1st century BC and the beginning of the 5th century AD, roughly corresponding to Roman domination of Egypt. Although this is a very late period in Egyptian history, cultural and religious traditions had persisted to a remarkable degree in this small community far removed from the centres of power.

The excavations (still in progress) of the necropolis have uncovered more than 700 bodies in either a mummified or a skeletal state. Careful examination of the skeletons has revealed that as a general rule these too bear traces of mummification. The poor condition of these human remains is due to systematic pillaging and – since the necropolis lies right alongside the fields – flooding from irrigation canals. The skeletons have been studied according to classical osteometric methods, but the presence of a fair number of mummies in a satisfactory condition led to the idea of carrying out radiological studies on site. By looking in this way at a homogeneous series (the first time this had occurred) it was possible to establish a cross-section of an entire population – a very different situation from investigating mummies in museums.

The complete X-ray process had thus to be carried out in a desert location with no electricity or running water, a feat achieved by using a traditional portable machine connected up to the site generator. The developing lab posed more of a problem, but the final results were comparable to negatives produced by standard procedures.

Most of the mummies have been stripped of their bandages and ornaments and many are encrusted with sand and require careful cleaning to prevent artifacts appearing on the X-rays. The clean-up operation is followed by a clinical description, and a series of photographs is taken to show comparative measurements. Then the X-rays are taken – at least eight negatives in each case to cover all the different parts of the body, with particular attention to the skull, and further negatives for any area that seems of particular interest.... In some cases samples of hair, nails, skin, resin and embalming products are taken for analysis. When all these various procedures have been completed the mummies, duly labelled, are placed in tombs that have been selected for their security and ease of access.

Results

...These findings show that at Duch we are dealing with a population of Mediterranean type, of slim build and average height (men 1.65 m, women 1.55 m), pale skinned....almost identical in feature to the populations of the Nile valley.

Pathological evidence is fairly extensive. In several cases there is evidence of a fatal fracture resulting from trauma: in one case, for example, an old woman died from a fracture to the thighbone; in another, a child died as a result of a fractured skull. Of 38 adults X-rayed, 74% were suffering from osteoarthritis of the spinal column – an unusually high percentage probably attributable to manual labour – and a further 84% were suffering from scoliosis. Striae relating to arrested growth were observed in almost two thirds of cases (practically double Gray's figure), indicating fairly frequent

periods of food shortage. Parasitic illnesses still encountered in Egypt today, such as filariasis and in particular bilharzia, were also identified. But despite the overall state of health of the population, which can only be described as poor, the average lifespan (not taking into account perinatal mortality, which must have been very high) was 38. Mummification appears to have been virtually universal. Mummies represent about two fifths of the total human remains, but artifacts characteristic of mummification are indicated for the majority of skeletons. Deterioration was due to the poor conditions in which the mummies were conserved and, contrary to popular opinion, the quality of the mummification itself was good. Although abdominal evisceration was rare, removal of the brain was very common, occurring in 33 out of 51 skulls studied, in other words 65% of cases. Differences in the construction of the mummies show that Herodotus' description of the different categories of treatment, from the most rudimentary to the most elaborate, continued to hold good even at this late date. The most elaborate treatment involved gilding the body and in particular the face. The study of mummies thus supplements that of funerary goods as a means of gauging the relative wealth of different tombs. It also provides evidence for the existence of social differentiation within a population which has otherwise supplied us with scant written information.

F. Dunand and R. Lichtenberg, 1991

FURTHER READING

Adams, B., *Egyptian Mummies*, 1984

Aldred, C., *Egypt to the End of the Old Kingdom*, 1965

—, *Egyptian Art*, 1980

—, *The Egyptians*, 1987

Andrews, C., *Egyptian Mummies*, 1984

—, *Ancient Egyptian Jewellery*, 1990

—, *Amulets of Ancient Egypt*, 1994

Athanasi, G. d' *Researches and Discoveries in Upper Egypt under the Direction of Henry Salt Esq.*, 1836

Bakry, H.S., *A Brief Study of Mummies and Mummification*, 1965

Belzoni, G., *Narrative of the Operations and Recent Discoveries within the Pyramids, Temples and Tombs...*, 1820

Budge, E.A.W., *The Book of the Dead*, 1899

—, *The Mummy*, 1925, repr. 1987

Clayton, P.A., *The Rediscovery of Ancient Egypt: Artists and Travellers in the 19th Century*, 1982

—, *Chronicle of the Pharaohs*, 1994

Cockburn, A. and E., *Mummies, Disease and Ancient Cultures*, 1980

David, A.R., *Mysteries of the Mummies*, 1978

—, *The Ancient Egyptians, Religious Beliefs and Practices*, 1982

David, A.R., *et al.*, *The Manchester Museum Mummy Project*, 1979

Dawson, W.R. and P.H.K. Gray, *Catalogue of Egyptian Antiquities in the British Museum: I Mummies and Human Remains*, 1968

Dawson, W.R. and E.P. Uphill, *Who Was Who in Egyptology*, 2nd ed., 1972

Dunand, F., and R. Lichtenberg, 'Les momies de la nécropole de Douch', *Archéologia*, No. 240, November 1988

El Mahdy, C., *Mummies, Myth and Magic*, 1991

Faulkner, R.O., *The Egyptian Pyramid Texts*, 1969

—, *The Egyptian Coffin Texts*, 1973–7

—, *The Ancient Egyptian Book of the Dead*, 1985

Fleming, S., *et al.*, *The Egyptian Mummy: Secrets and Science*, 1980

Gardiner, A.H., *The Attitude of the Ancient Egyptians to Death and the Dead*, 1935

Goyon, J.-C., *Rituels funéraires de l'ancienne Egypte*, 1972

Gray, P.H.K., *Radiological Aspects of the Mummies of Ancient Egyptians in the Rijksmuseum van Oudheden*, OMRO, 47, 1966

—, 'Radiography of Ancient Egyptian Mummies', *Medical Radiography and Photography*, 4, 1967

Hamilton-Peterson, J., and C. Andrews, *Mummies: Death and Life in Ancient Egypt*, 1978

Harris, J.E., and Weeks, K.R., *X-Raying the Pharaohs*, 1973

Harris, J.E., and Wente, E., *An X-Ray Atlas of the Royal Mummies*, 1980

Hobson, C., *Exploring the World of the Pharaohs*, 1987

James, T.G.H. *Ancient Egypt, the Land and its Legacy*, 1979

Lurker, M., *The Gods and Symbols of Ancient Egypt: an Illustrated Dictionary*, 1982

Mayer, L., *Views in Egypt*, 1804

Montet, P., *Eternal Egypt*, 1964

Mummies and Magic: The Funerary Arts of Ancient Egypt, Boston Exhibition Catalogue, 1988

Peet, T.E., *The Great Tomb Robberies of the Twentieth Egyptian Dynasty*, 1930

Quirke, S., *Ancient Egyptian Religion*, 1992

Reeves, N., *The Complete Tutankhamun*, 1990

Smith, G.E. and Dawson, W.R., *Egyptian Mummies*, 1924, repr.1991

Spencer, A.J., *Death in Ancient Egypt*, 1982

Taylor, J., *Egyptian Coffins*, 1989

Vercoutter, J. *The Search for Ancient Egypt*, 1992

Zandee, J., *Death as an Enemy According to Ancient Egyptian Conceptions*, 1960

LIST OF ILLUSTRATIONS

INDEX

PHOTO CREDITS

ACL, Brussels 37r. All rights reserved spine, 12, 13, 15a, 21a, 21b, 22a, 23, 34a, 41, 42a, 56, 58a, 59b, 70, 70–1, 72r, 79, 80l, 80r, 81, 86a, 91r, 92b, 94l, 96, 97, 100, 102, 104, 108, 109, 112, 113, 114, 116, 117. Bibliothèque Nationale, Paris 14, 17, 18–19, 32–3, 48–9, 52al, 63, 69a, 73, 74–5, 75a, 77, 78al, 103. Boston Museum of Fine Arts 98. British Museum, London 11, 28, 29a, 34–5, 47a, 47b, 50a, 68l. Dagli Orti, Paris 60a. Edimedia, Paris 33. Electa, Milan 29b, 54–5. FMR/Franco Lovera 43a. J.L. Heim 92a, 93bl. IFAO/Alain Leclerc, Paris 74a. J. Liepe, Berlin 43r, 44b, 46b, 50b, 51r, 52b, 54–5, 62ar, 68r. Roger Lichtenberg 1–9, 36r, 76, 82a, 82b, 86b, 87a, 87b, 90, 91l, 93a, 93br, 118, 118–19. Musée de l'Homme, Paris 94r. Musée Guimet d'Histoire Naturelle, Lyons 27, 29c, 32, 35, 51l, 52ar, 53, 54–5, 89. Pelizaeus Museum, Hildesheim front cover: background, 26, 38r, 38b, 88–9. Réunion des Musées Nationaux, Paris back cover, 15b, 16, 22b, 30, 30–1, 34c, 36l, 37l, 38–9, 39, 40, 42–3, 44a, 45l, 46a, 54–5, 57, 60b, 61ar, 61b, 62al, 62b, 64–5, 65a, 66, 67l, 67r, 68–9, 101. Manchester Museum 20–1. Roger-Viollet, Paris 31, 35, 72l, 78ar, 78–9, 95, 107, 111. Stierlin/Artephot, Paris 24a, 24b, 24–5, 25. Sygma, Paris front cover, 83, 84–5.

TEXT CREDITS

Grateful acknowledgment is made for use of material from the following: (pp. 100–1) from *Voices from Ancient Egypt* by R.B. Parkinson, published by the British Museum Press, 1991; (p. 101) from *Egyptian Mummies* by G. Elliot Smith and Warren R. Dawson, courtesy of Kegan Paul International, London and New York; (pp. 104–5) from *Death in Ancient Egypt* by A.J. Spencer, published by Penguin Books, 1982; (pp. 114–15) reprinted courtesy Eastman Kodak Company.

The authors wish to thank M. Jean-Louis de Cenival, head curator of the Egyptian Antiquities Department at the Louvre and Mme Marie-France Aubert, curator of the same, the Institut Français d'Archéologie Orientale team and Alain Leclerc, photographer with the IFAO; M. Luc Limme, curator of Egyptian antiquities at the Musée Royal in Brussels; Mme Marie-Françoise Audouard at Editions du Chêne; M. Roland Mourer, curator at the Musée Guimet d'Histoire Naturelle in Lyons.

Françoise Dunand, Ph.D.,
is professor of the history of religion at the
University of Strasbourg-II. A former member of the
Institut Français d'Archéologie Orientale in Cairo, she
has published a number of books and articles on late
Egyptian religious beliefs and practices. Since 1983 she
has been directing archaeological excavations at the
necropolis at Duch, in the Kharga Oasis, on behalf of
the IFAO.

Roger Lichtenberg
is a doctor of medicine and director of the radiology
unit at the Institut Arthur-Vernes in Paris. He was a
member of the team that examined the mummy of
Ramesses II in Paris in 1976 and has written a number
of articles on clinical radiology and the study of
mummies. Since 1982 he has been in charge of X-raying
and conducting anthropological and palaeopathological
studies on the mummies of Duch.

*To all our colleagues on the Duch excavations and to the
Egyptian workmen who helped us in our explorations.*

© Gallimard 1991

English translation © Thames and Hudson Ltd,
London, 1994

Translated by Ruth Sharman

British Library Cataloguing-in-Publication Data

A catalogue record for this book is available from
the British Library

ISBN 0–500–30045–3

Printed and bound in Italy
by Editoriale Libraria, Trieste